Heavenly Rose
Angel in Disguise

ISBN   978-1955728027 print; 978-1955728034 epub

Dedication

To the one who chose me—to honor till death do us part
Pamela Diane Rose Timmons Kaniut.

Acknowledgements

This project is the result of dozens of people who know Pam and to them I am grateful.

For those I was unable to contact I apologize.

Jody Winquist at Northern Printing infused her artistic creativity and formatted this book.

Compiled by Larry Kaniut

Table of Contents

INTRODUCTION

CHILDHOOD

YOUTH

COLLEGE CLASSMATES

MARRIAGE & KIDS

YOUNG PEOPLE

CHURCH

TEACHERS-COLLEAGUES

NEIGHBORS

OTHERS

FAMILY

ACTIVITIES

CARDS

MISCELLANEOUS

LETTERS AND MISSIVES

PAM SAYS

PAMISMS

PAM'S HAPPY MARRIAGE RECIPE

PAM'S FUNERAL ARRANGEMENT

INDEX

Introduction

The impetus for this project was inspiration—because of Pam's longstanding health issues, I thought I could collect people's comments about her and give them to her as a way of inspiring her in her times of discouragement or pain. However since that beginning I've realized the project would be a testimony to her, more than an encouragement for her. It will stand as a bit of bio and a tribute to her character and behavior, something for her children and grandchildren as well as for friends and neighbors. I may have begun it around 1976.

Format of comments: family, friends, neighbors, school mates—elementary through college, roommates (Joy and Calling Lake), church, co-worker…most all of whom became friends at the least.

Portland, Oregon. Warner Pacific College. Fall 1960. Two hot chicks walking up the maple tree lined sidewalk on 68th in front of the college library. These two goddesses captured his full attention, he being an athletic college freshman. He focused on the shorter one clad in a red and white plaid skirt, her waist length auburn hair in a pony tail bobbing behind. He decided to learn more about this hazel-eyed beauty.

Within a few months his brother-in-law and sister invited him to drive to Mt. Hood with them and suggested he bring a date. Oh, my.

The girl from Dayton, Oregon—the auburn haired beauty—accepted. He found out later the date was a bust for her. However the next eight months he determined this woman was the one he wanted to spend his life with.

She captivated me from the beginning. Pamela Diane Timmons. Eighteen years old. Five feet two. Hazel eyes. A single pony tail of auburn hair trailing below her waist. She was a college frosh, a co-ed at Warner Pacific in Portland, Oregon. A farm girl come to the big city to attend college and to get her man. A tomboy and a flirt.

She had a palomino gelding named Duke. Seventeen hands high. Used to haul downed aircraft from the forest.

Pam and Crystal in work clothes.

Childhood

Hazel Timmons (Pam's mother) On March 31, 2001

I received a phone call and the following email info from Michael Timmons, Pam's nephew. He had worked with Hazel and sent a scanned version in her handwriting which I transcribed into print.

From Hazel via Michael December 22, 2001

Pam was just a sweet, lovely baby—when Uncle George had breakfast, she would slide along the bench up to him and stick her finger in the butter plate and eat some. Very independent.

Went to meet her brother and sister from school not waiting for her mother.

At school one day she went home with one of her classmates and didn't take the bus home as she was suppose to.

She was most interested in horses and animals.

No problems in high school.

Liked the farm.

A very sweet, loving child.

A very special mother—the family shows the results.

Pam was born January 21, 1942. She was a much loved baby girl. After they married, John and Velma Rutz, Howard's sister, came to live in our basement because places to live were hard to get since there had been a war going on. John often stopped and played with Pam—usually if it was a nice day and I had her out in our buggy. Velma was jealous of her—they didn't have any children so John always played with her. And if he got to hold her at a dinner table, he would feed her things that she wasn't ready for—but she managed just fine.

In those days since I didn't have a car, I would put the babies in the buggy and we would walk the two oldest—Pep and Pat—to school up on 33rd Avenue. We lived a block off 42nd at 43rd and Ainsworth. One day she didn't wait for me but started out on her own. When I got to 42nd street, I saw her way up ready to turn on Emerson Street, where the school was. A man going down 42nd took her hand and brought her to me—she had told him that I was her mother. She was safe because we didn't have all the problems that we have now. And I thanked the man and proceeded to go back to meet Pep and Pat.

Then one time—she was much older and went out to ride her horse with the girl next door. Pam liked horses. Marcia and she shared a room. Pam had cut out some pictures from some magazines and left a mess in her room. Marcia came down crying that Pam had a mess and that she had made a line between the beds and wasn't going to clean it up. So I sent Pam up. At first she wouldn't go but I cut off a little limb and switched her legs.

I have never forgotten the fact that I hurt her. I think it hurt me more than it hurt her. And she went up to the room and all she did was push all the papers under her bed—at least the room looked very nice. I'm sure we discussed the situation when she came home that evening—other than that I haven't anything more. Oh, yes, I have, she rode her horse in a neighborhood fair one summer.

Duke was the best horse…Duke got sick and we called in a vet who said he was too far gone. So he put him to sleep. What a sad day that was, not a dry eye on anyone.

Pam went to the same college that I graduated from. She was working on a special degree—first grade teacher. I watched her work with her children. She would have become a very good teacher, but she, like myself, never got to hold down a position.

Pam was independent but she was also a very kind and thoughtful person. She came down to Oregon when I had my stroke (in 1999?) and every day she came to cheer me up—did all kinds of nice things, read articles, etc. Then she invited me to come up to Anchorage last year (summer 2000). She was helping—helped me up bathe and dress and even washed my hair, set it and could style it too and then every night she tucked me into bed. She is not only good to me, sending letters, cookies and calling almost every day, many of her friends tell about her thoughtfulness and TLC to them too. She is one special person and should be honored.

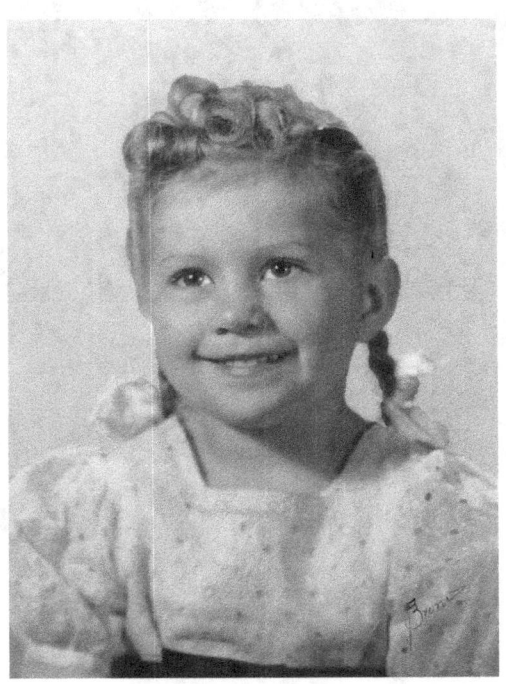

Pam and Trigger

Youth

Lynn Stuart, May 2, 2016 letter

The Timmons family in total were extremely instrumental in guiding me as a young man and Pam was always just a bit more special and I would say that is because she was always happy and ready to accommodate visitors and friends of the Timmons family. She loved riding horses and spent a lot of time on them as I recall. I do not recall any special names for her…just Pam.

Lynn A. Stuart

A gift of 70 years a letter from Pam to her older brother Howard (Pepper)

Growing up on Ainsworth Street you enjoyed father's ducks in the round pond, seeing gooseberries grow on mom's bushes and had plenty of room for your friends to play. You boys had a club and you chose me, six years younger, to be the mascot.

At 13, moving over to 112th you kept active walking to school, rowing our boat and swimming. By the edge of the lake Dad built the long water slide and gym set for us to enjoy. I think you kept far away from my horse, dad's pigs and you never tried to take away my milking duties.

During high school mother kept you company on your daily runs. It seems like from the lake house we heard you barking football orders. Sitting on bleachers at the high school we were so nervous watching you and Tommy wrestle. About this time you and Pat headed off as clowns for the church Halloween party. I'm not sure you made it because of a car wreck. Were you driving with the shoe boxes you left home in?

As we headed home from Holliday Park Church, Dad spoiled us with a stop at the Dairy Queen. Mom's Sunday rolls were huge and warm and we could count on a beef roast. Lynn, George and Don enjoyed many meals of our steak and huge batches of homemade ice-cream...and quickly did away with part of mom's weekly 9 loaves of bread. We must have assumed everyone ate like we did.

Dad's pigs loved him so much they followed him up the steps trying to get into the kitchen. Dad kept loving animals even after one of his steers rammed him with its horns.

You were such a sweet, older brother—taking me to the city wide roller skating before I was old enough to go.

Standing in the kitchen one morning before school I wouldn't leave you alone. So you grabbed the hot cake turner and left that flat shape on the back of my coat.

You left us for the U of Oregon. It was hard to have you leave us. George moved into your bedroom. It wasn't long before the fire department came after Craig unwittingly caught the covers on fire. Dad was busy growing mushrooms in the long dark shed. He let George work on his roadster car. Dad and I started dreaming and searching for my property.

Then came the summers you worked long, long hours but squeezed getting to know Dot into your work week—getting home at terribly late hours.

My heart broke when Dot took you away from me. I cried and cried—an emotional teenager (what a lot of happiness, wonderful children, fun and excitement she brought into your life).

You and Dot joined us at the farm one hot summer when the temperatures were 112. Ice cream, huge meals, swimming and pop from Catherine's store added fun to the huge job of building the grain elevator. About 12 of us kept at it day after day.

We were all so proud watching you graduate that special day in Eugene. I think I was wearing a pink dress that I adored (Dot gave it to me. She was so thoughtful to pass on so many things to me).

It was great fun visiting you both in California and seeing little Kevin in his crib. I wanted to steal him. Your lovely home was like a movie set. In shorts I walked down the sidewalk of your street, dodging Palm branches as it snowed. You showed us the huge computer and explained your work.

Then, back to Oregon you and Dot came, building amazing-wonderful homes as your children kept arriving. You advanced from a good job to a better job—to an even better job—becoming the kind of boss and father and husband that will cause God one day to say, "Well done!"

Pam as May Queen   *College 1960*

Pam on Duke

College Classmates

Lorin W. Myers, March 21, 1996 letter

Dear Larry,

I consider it a privilege to write a few comments about your dear little wife Pam. Prior to the fall of 1995 I would have had to say that I knew her way back in the early 60's and had not had the privilege to meet either of you for almost 30 years, but it was good to be in your home and to share even the brief time that we had being blessed by your and Pam's hospitality.

I only knew Pam for brief time, and that was while we were both students at Warner Pacific College in Portland, Oregon. I remember her as a bubbly cute girl who was shorter than me, and that made her "interesting" to say the least. She seemed to be active on campus, but disappeared on weekends as best I can remember. In a class or two that we shared she had a sweet spirit about her, and I enjoyed being in small group discussions with her and others who were different from me the California guy who had been in the Marine Corps, had attended the University of California at Berkeley of all places, and was not really sure why I was at Warner Pacific at that time.

In closing then I remember Pam "Timmons" as a neat girl that I would have liked to know better.

Sincerely yours,
Lorin W. Myers

11

Gary LaRay Smith, April 23, 1997 letter

Words and thoughts are scattered. She will endure in three neat kids. Children the Lord blessed you both with. Think of what Lekander said thirty years ago—only in God's view of Pam.

Weston Gray, Nov. 17, 2016 letter

I met Larry and Pam Kaniut at Warner Pacific College in Portland, Oregon.

I started dating Pam's sister, Marcia Timmons. On the weekends, sometimes I was invited to the Timmons' estate near McMinnville, Oregon. The Timmons clan would gather and enjoy each other's company. Larry's wife, Pam, was one of the most kind persons I had ever met. Her gentle ways was one of her strengths. The family loved to tease each other a lot. Pam would laugh and sometimes just shake her head in the fun that was going amongst the family and outsiders.

Larry and Pam chose to move to Anchorage, Alaska. My friendship continued through telephone calls. During their time in Alaska, Pam got ill and became very weak, as well. During the telephone calls when I got to speak with her, Pam never complained. In due time she got well and was able to continue her daily life as a wife and mother to her family.

Pam has a strong faith in her Lord and Savior in spite of what life brings her way. She is a true example of what it means to be a Christian, and live it each day God gives her a new day to live for Him.

Thank you for allowing me to be a friend to Larry and Pam (Timmons) Kaniut since our college days.

Sincerely, Weston Gray Visalia, CA

Gene Amondson, February 4, 2005 email

(Gene prefaced his email with "Larry's wife has suffered for years and he wanted a word about her, so this is what I sent"):

The Lovely Girl in Alaska named Pam
That sweet little girl called Pam I know

12

From Alaska and Portland, so long ago.
She's giving. She's kind. Her heart's full of joy, that we all
  know....
I ask how she has been fashioned so.

Was it the Larry she lives with...
The kids that she's had or
The loss of her sister?
Was it parents or maybe the farm?
The days in bed, the suffering so?
What did it? We many never know.
But God had a hand in it...yes. That we all know.

Pam, the next time I am in Alaska, I will sing you the song we
  sang each year to our kids, using their name:
Pam's so special
Oh, so special.
God gave her to us
That is why we love her so.

Gene

Joyce Amstutz, May 1996 letter

In the fall of 1962 I attended Oregon College of Education at Monmouth. Without having accommodation at the college arranged for previous to arrival, I was delighted to find a place where a Christian girl was living by herself. She was open to a roommate so we agreed to put "Pam Timmons and Joyce Stauffer" on the door.

Pam was my kind of friend—and I felt comfortable from the start with her as a roommate. She loved the Lord and secondly was pleasant to live with. There was a peacefulness about living in the same apartment. I felt I experienced her dedication to the Christian graces and she sought to do all within her ability to make our year pleasant.

Pam's consideration for the comfort and welfare of others stood out to me. She and I could appreciate the needed quiet in the mornings for our private devotions. It was just amazing how God

13

brought us together when we had never known one another before. Our goals were very similar and we enjoyed cooking together. It was shared and mutual respect for each other.

Pam always seemed to have a level-headed sensitivity to situations. She could keep herself attractive without overdoing it because she was beautiful from within.

Pam and I met again after we were both married when she and Larry were on their way to Alaska to set up housekeeping. We were living at Calling Lake, Alberta at the time. That visit was very special. Then over the years Pam faithfully sent family pictures and letter updates on life in the far north. She would tell of her health problem and severe limitations but always mentioning areas of thanksgiving. Always we were made aware of the specialness of their family. Years later in 1993, Pam saw to it that we were included in the homeward trip from Oregon to Alaska. Again we had a special time of sharing.

It seems appropriate to close with a prayer of thanksgiving:

Thank You Lord for friendship

For Love You give that is real

Alberta to Oregon was a long trip

Your love Lord Pam and I could feel.

Marriage and kids

Larry Writes

When I came home from school in 1967, Pam told me we were going to have a baby. When I asked her if were the mailman or the plumber, she told me it was the TV repairman. Since we didn't have a TV, I knew she was fibbin'…but that's not the only reason.

From family journal about our kids:

I'm babysitting for Pam who is at a church missionary meeting. I thought it was awfully quiet. I just changed Jill and left the Vasoline (clue) on the floor. I checked the girls' room and…guess whom I found in their Mayflower fort Vasolining a doll? Both gooey girls. I asked Gin just who gave her permission to play there with the Vasoline, and she replied, "I gived I-self permission. I wanted I-self to play with the bass-o-line." Later, after lovingly chewing her out, I told her she could play with the Vasoline only if mommy or daddy wanted her to or if she asked either if she would. She happily asked, "Can I play with the bass-o-line, Dad?" So much for that lesson. 11/31-71

3-22-72   Pam has been working with the girls with the names of the apostles. She asked Gin to tell me the names of the apostles during their Bible story time. Ginger said, "Thomas, Peter, Jamie and Kim." (Jamie and Kim are cousins)

Pam Writes

I took the girls out to the mailbox in the wagon (located at 140th and DeArmoun, 4 blocks from our house—on a long set up of boards and posts with another 3-4 dozen)—about two weeks ago. Gordon and Larry Best were working to drain some spring runoff and some chuck holes. We stopped to help then started out again. I hit a hole dumping the girls onto the ground—Ginger landed on the snow covered road, and Jill slipped headfirst into a snow melted water puddle, soaking herself.   5-11-72

Our electricity was off almost three hours today. We had taken a few minutes to ask God to help our electricity come on soon. We had enjoyed our candle light time, but finally I put Jill in bed. Shortly the lights came on. Ginger ran to tell Jill in the bedroom then calmly walked down the hall saying, "Thank God."   1-28-73

Larry Writes

Pam is narrating the Noah/ark story with the girls. Gin has a baby blanket on her head to look like Noah. Jill is spraying water on her head from the empty Avon "cabin" bottle. This spray represents falling rain. Pretty soon Noah sends out a bird—a yellow plastic one—and the ark lands on a large mountain. Noah and the animals are safe, and the girls pray.   3-18-74

In 1970 we needed to plug a hole in our wall, originally designed to be a fireplace. Turns out Gil Perry saved our bacon. He devoted ten days to our needs during which time Pam fed him lunch and dinner. He was a mason earning $9.95 an hour and we managed to get his expertise after which he said he "didn't want to charge us too much" and wondered "if $250 was too much?" Pam was her traditional self and cheerfully fed Gil as well as our two daughters under the age of 2 and a non-skilled masonry husband.

Young People

Over the years even before our marriage Pam has had a huge effect upon young people, from Larry King and cousins, Dave Compton, Helen and Toby Bell, Vickie Wilson, Louie Jensen and countless others from the 1960's through 2017 where she has loved and catered to little neighbor girls and boys—Larry and Sue Best, Dana and Beth Kucera, Chris and Derek Snyder, Katie and Bruce Goerisch, Charlene, and Cathy Nippel, Lynette and Heidi Baer, the Hammans— Ron, Chris Andy and Ruth, Grant and Katie Kaiser, the  Wilkisons—Ivan, Salina and Janeal, Kenny Perkins, Cindy and Christie Stevenson, Darin and Troy Nibert, Carrie Gerondale, Shandy, the Davis girls—Anne, Mary Kay, Joanna, Rachel's daughter and son, Tasia Tuttle and brother Trey and cousin Jaylin and brother Jaxson.

Some might compare Pam's compassion with taking in strays however they weren't strays but someone who needed support or "loving up," as she would say. In 1967 we took in Louie Jensen, a ninth grade Oregon student whose mother thought a year with us would be good for him. In 1972 we took in Tom Bentley so he could finish his senior year in high school and not have to go to Texas with his Air Force family. Charlene Nippell was a neighbor girl who needed some housing as was Tracy Blair for the summer of 1992, a college friend of our daughter Jill. In 1985 we housed Cal Pappas, a teaching colleague for the summer. From 2016-2017 our older daughter Ginger and husband Brad and daughter Sarah lived with us for six months after they had a house fire; and from 2016 to 2017 they lived with us again while making the transition to their new home.

During that same time span Pam took it upon herself to send many a letter or note or surprise to one of those kids—one who needed encouragement or a lift…or, some spending money

James Jody Keasler, Facebook 2/15/2018

Pam was always quiet and she and my mother always talked. When I first met you and Pam I was a young child. M y parents took us over to that garage apartment when you first moved to Alaska. The second vivid memory was one time, again younger, we came over to your house for dinner and Pam had her hair down and I've only seen it in the bun. When I saw how long it was and I was always impressed. And the last thing was that I remember Pam was the only person that I knew that made wild game meat taste like a Gourmet meal. I have high regard for my mother's cooking but she couldn't even master game like Pam.

Dann L. Pierce, June 25, 1996 letter

Dear Larry,

This is in response to your January note concerning memories of Pam in your life.

I have clear memories of visiting your house as a high school junior or senior. Four or five high school boys would invade your place for an evening of storytelling, card playing (ROOK!), and general tom foolery. All of this would have been laudable, but unremarkable had the house we visited been a conventional size. Memories can play tricks, but I recall the Kaniut house on Arctic Blvd. as being quite spacious (if compared to a phone booth). How Pam put up with the raucous—probably predictable and banal—talk (not to mention the laughter, and noise) is hard (in retrospect) to understand; at the time it seemed all very normal and fun. Her patience and hospitality greatly contributed (both at this Arctic Blvd. house and later up on the hill - before we knew it was Natrona!) to the acceptance and maturation of teens who always need both.

Thanks, Pam

Lynette Baer c. 1985 ? high school class assignment

My memories are colorful and vivid. Her blue house sat on a large lot, covered thickly with trees. The huge stone chimney rose into the sky and a hazy steady stream of smoke could always be seen emerging from it. The brightly stained glass front door had a hand painted welcome sign hanging on it, welcoming the world to come in.

I can remember going to her house. The warm aroma of fresh baked goods always welcomed me. Her south facing, sunny bay window was where I would sit and listen to her tell me about the "old days."

She was a sickly lady, since I can remember. Bedridden, most of the day, except for the short twenty minutes every hour that she could stand on her fragile, slippered feet.

She is the one that discovered the creativeness in me, like an archaeologist uncovering an ancient trunk of priceless jewels.

I can sharply recall the special afternoons that I would spend at her house. She was my second mom. A mother and wife herself, she accepted me as one of her own.

After school I would go and do crafts with her. On spring days she would have chocolate milk and cookies waiting for me and on cold days it would be hot chocolate. She loved nature and we would make bird feeders out of huge pine cones. We would fill them with peanut butter, dip them in bird seed and hang them on the spruce trees outside her bay window. Her kindness toward all, animals and humans alike, radiated from her actions. Even though she was ill, she did more good things in her life than any average person could even hope to do.

Her love towards God, nature and people has touched me and I still look to her as a perfect role model.

Randal Terry, Apr 18, 2016 (1 day ago)

I could write a book on Pam myself. I'll share a few of my memories that I probably shared before.

When I first come to know Pam, the Kaniut family was living on Artic Blvd. in a small one bedroom house. Ginger was newly born. I would come over with other former wrestlers and spend the night playing Rook. Every now and then, Pam would come out of the back room (her hair in a bun) to grab something and go back in with Ginger. It took years before I knew she could talk. I remember on one occasion when she came out of the back room, her hair way hanging almost to the floor and I was in awe, not knowing how she could get all that hair in the small bun.

Eventually, the Kaniut family had built a house in the boondocks. I was riding with the Kaniut family in his VW station wagon, returning from church I think, and I started singing with the song on the radio and I stopped, as Tony James would do, and said, "I bet you thought I was the radio," and to my surprise, Pam says, "Yes, the static!" I almost fell out of your car onto your dirt road laughing. One, because she said something very funny and two, to my surprise, I found out that Pam had a voice and every since then, she hasn't stopped talking.

I can remember all the meals I have had at the Kaniut house and I love eating there for Pam was a great cook. She could make anything taste great (probably even liver which I hate). I remember one such meal, I was seating there looking at what I thought was a pot roast (wrapped up with the strings that a roast would normally have) and after eating a great meal, Pam asked if I like the meat and I told her I did. She asked me if I knew what I just ate and I told her, roast. She laughs and says I just ate moose heart.

In my observations through the years, I could honestly say that Pam has a heavenly soul about her. I have seen her walk among the animals and they would come right up to her without fear and even protect her. I believe that the bears that appear in your yard wouldn't harm her is she got stuck in the yard when one appeared.

Ginger, Jill and Ben are a great testament of what a wonder lady Pam is. Without using physical punishment, she raised three great kids who exhibit some of her traits. She did that through love.

Bedtime now. May write more later.

Take care

Dale Steele

I was in elementary school when I first met you, Pam and Larry. My family and yours participated in the same church. But it wasn't until Junior High that I got to know both of you. You invited me into your lives. You became like an uncle and aunt. We have remained in that relationship all of these years.

It has always been a joy to enter your home, Pam. I guess because of the many times I have been included in your family's life, pulling up a chair by your kitchen fire always warms me like being "home". I remember learning how to remove clams from their shells in your kitchen sink, clean hooligan at 3 a.m., the extra warmth of splitting firewood just outside your window, and "cheating" at Rook under the mirrored ceiling over your dining room table. I enjoyed many a meal in your home. Story after story we shared in the warmth of your fireplace, then, memory after memory—the kind that refocus one's faith, purpose and foundations. Your kitchen has always been a place of holy communion for me—a place of holy hospitality for which I will always be grateful. It's a place of love, laughter and even a few tears. It is your love for Jesus, your family, and the many friends you treat like family, that make it that way.

Thank you for living in steadfast faith in the midst of trials. Thanks for sharing that faith so genuinely in the everyday-ness of life. Thanks for being the beautiful person God made you to be and letting all of us experience Jesus in you.

--Dale Steele, DMin. March 2018.

Roy and Joyce Mullen, April 18, 2005 letter

Roy told me he was talking with Pam one day when visiting and made the comment, "We have to go to church." Pam, in her wisdom spoke up and said, "You don't have to go to church, you get to go to church!" That was spoken with a great perspective, since we have such freedom to worship when others don't, and sometimes we take it for granted. I'm sure she was also thinking about having the health and strength to be able to attend church. Thanks Pam!

We would call Pam the Angel of Hospitality since the Lord has made it so evident this is her gift. Pam, you have always made us feel so welcome, like we were royalty. You have a wonderful way of making others feel important and loved by the undivided attention you give. You are also a fabulous cook and we appreciate the time and energy you take to make such delicious food for your guests.

We would also note Pam's generosity of sharing her time, energy and food. She is so giving. One time I mentioned I didn't have a butter knife and when our visit was over and we were ready to leave she gave us a butter knife and goodies she had baked to take with us. That really touched my heart. Thanks Pam and thanks Larry for allowing your wife to be so generous. You allow her to exercise the gifts God has blessed her with.

Love always, Roy and Joyce.

Janel Knisley Smith, June 4, 1996 letter

Hi Larry,

I like the title A Rose Petal from Heaven (thank you for thinking of me. I feel honored)

Jill is a treasure in my life...very dear to my heart. Even though we live miles apart I still feel close to her and know I always will. Jill's eyes have always sparkled with Jesus. She is genuinely kind and gentle and sweet spirited, always lifting another up and above herself and humbly serving with all of her heart...adventurous, she's willing to be silly and has a roaring sense of humor—the best friend anyone could ever have!

I think back on our childhood and there was always a distant figure watching, listening, encouraging, laughing with (or at us)...a gentle, quiet spirit, leading us as an example of a Christian woman, wife, mother and friend. I believe I owe the quality of Jill and my friendship to Pam. The role model of Pam is evident in her children—even her children's friends—as I often think about Pam now that I am a wife and mother. Her combination of grace, beauty, gentleness, genuine concern, care and love...always quick to smile... "she is clothed with strength and dignity, she can laugh at the days to come. She speaks with wisdom and faithful instruction is on her tongue. She watches over the affairs of her household and does not eat the bread of idleness...a woman who fears the Lord should be praised." A wife of noble character. Proverbs 31: 24-30

Thank you, Pam for the blessing you have been in my life in so many ways. "Her children will rise up and call her blessed."

Kim Miller Ingraham, May 25, 1996 letter

It's been tough to sit down and try to put into words what or who Pam Kaniut is. Turn to the concordance in your Bible—look up gentleness, faithfulness, kindness, loving...any of the verses referenced can apply to her. I particularly like Philippians 4:4-7: "Rejoice in the Lord always. I will say it again: Rejoice! Let your gentleness be evident to all. The Lord is near. Do not be anxious about anything but in everything, by prayer and petition, with thanksgiving, present your requests to God. And the peace of God, which transcends all understanding, will guard your hearts and minds in Christ Jesus."

Mrs. Kaniut personifies these verses. Her gentle spirit is easily seen. My memories of the Kaniut house mostly focus around the kitchen where she'd often be sitting, just sharing conversation. Just being around her let me experience an environment filled with acceptance and love.

I consider it quite an honor to know her—to have had the chance to know her specialness. You know our Father must look down on Pam Kaniut and smile at the fine example she has set for all about being a devoted child of God.

Love, Kim Miller Ingraham

David, Pam, Cherlyn and Ryan Thibault, March 4, 1996 letter

We would be honored to say what Pam Kaniut has meant to us. I have known Pam and Larry and their sweet family since my family moved to Anchorage and attended First Church of God in 1971. David started attending First Church of God 1 in 1975 when he got to know and love the Kaniut family.

Pam and Larry were very influential and helped me and David as teenagers in the youth group at First Church. We know they helped all the youth and had all of us over to their house for many activities. We learned a lot and enjoyed being with the Kaniut family.

Pam has always been my role model and mentor. I have admired her for many years and value her ideas and opinions. Pam is a great counselor and the best person to ask advice! Pam is very sweet, loving, kind, compassionate, gentle, understanding, and patient. She is one of the few women who truly desires to be Godly and God has answered her prayer.

Pam has done an excellent job of doing everything God requires from us such as teaching and raising our family; praying for ourselves, family, friends, and all others; helping and loving others; and following His will for our lives. We will never understand why God has allowed Pam to be sick for so long but we know that the time we spend on this earth is very short in any case and only what is done for God will last.

Pam is one of the very few people in this world who truly follows God and we love her very much. She has meant a lot to all of us and our lives are much more beautiful because of her. We continue to pray for health and strength for Pam and know she is in the center of God's will and He will take care of her and reward her greatly for her faithfulness, love, commitment, devotion, and thankfulness to God. All praise belongs to God who gives us strength, power, love and His spirit.

Love, David, Pam, Cheryl and Ryan Thibault

Eugene Greenfield email: March 9, 2018

It was a beautiful winter day in 1976-77 when I was invited to go sledding after church. This was my first opportunity to do some real sledding since I just moved up from Oklahoma. The only people I truly remember from that adventure were Larry and Pam. I remember lots of laughter and fun sliding down the hill on a shovel, or an inner-tube or if I was really lucky, an actual sled. After our sledding adventures we all went back to the house for hot cocoa and snacks and that was when I first truly got to know Pam and the entire family.

That winter was also when we had game night at First Church and I remember many, many hours playing ping-pong with Larry while Pam supervised the games. What truly amazed me and does to this day is how the love of Christ has always shown through her eyes. I always felt welcomed, loved and that I mattered when for so much of my life I wasn't sure. My life took a dark turn after I left the Navy and I struggled with addiction for many years. Yet even in those dark times when I would see Pam, there was always love offered from her and genuine gratitude that I mattered and that she truly cared for my well-being.

I could go on and on and on but suffice it to say that knowing Pam and her family has been one of the greatest blessings of my life to watch her walk through life and all the ups and downs with such grace and dignity; and to be allowed to call her friend is a blessing that God has granted me. I learned from her to face life with faith in Christ Jesus. I love you Pam; thank you for all of your years of praying for me.

Katie Goerisch Sturgell

Pam was my safe haven for when I couldn't go home. I remember doing dishes with her, playing softball in the backyard with the neighborhood, making and eating homemade ice cream (boy it took forever to make the ice cream) or curly fries, watching my horse get his stomach pumped, the lovely caramel popcorn balls on Halloween, coasting down DeArmoun with Larry to save on gas, and helping with the horses or playing with old Duke. There was always something interesting to do at your house. I learned a lot of lessons from Pam including patience, love, and perseverance through difficult medical conditions. Your house kept me sane!

I am so incredibly grateful to Pam for spending her time with me. Thank you, Pam, you made me a much better person! I honestly can't thank you enough! Your house has always been my ideal version of what my home should be.

I have a wonderful life now full of so many blessings I can't even begin to count them all. God has been very good to me. You couldn't have known what was going on in our home. I was very good at keeping secrets.

You two are amazing and man I am grateful for you in my life!

I love you forever and always,

Katie Goerisch Sturgell

Michael G. Edwards, March 19, 1996 letter

Dear Larry:

I appreciate you including me in this project. It means a lot to be able to contribute to this worthwhile project. Here's my submission:

I met Pam through her daughter Jill. Jill and I attended college together at George Fox in Newberg, Oregon in 1989-90. During the summers of 1990 and 1991 I came up to Alaska to work, and in 1990 when I told Jill at college that I was heading up to the Last Frontier to make "big bucks," she and I agreed to get together. I came over to Jill's place quite a bit on weekends and a few weeknights. After awhile I felt almost like family.

I remember Pam as a great mom, the kind of mom anyone would want to have. She was a hard worker with boundless energy, always making sure that everything around the house was just right. She was quite an entertainer. She knew just how to throw a party, have a barbeque, show off the geese, cheer you on in softball, or treat you to pizza. But more than that, in seeing the godliness her kids displayed (Jill reminded me of Christ's love every time we saw each other), I could see that she was more than just a fun mom. She instilled in her children the same sense of decency and uprightness she herself exuded.

After I married the summer of 1995, Pam sent my wife and I a nice wedding gift from the Kaniuts. The gesture speaks volumes of her as a thoughtful and caring person. I am very glad to have had her as a second mom while I was up in Alaska and that she still keeps in touch even though I'm no longer in the Last Frontier.

God bless, Michael G. Edwards

Beth and Rick Biel, June 10, 1996 letter

Dear Larry,

From Beth:

My earliest memory of Pam is when I would go over to her house to play with Ginger when she was just a toddler and I was about seven-years-old. Jill was just a tiny baby sitting in an infant seat. I remember Ginger showing her "love" towards Jill quite aggressively with huge hugs and shakes, and maybe even a bite or two. Pam was so gentle and would quietly tell Ginger how she should treat her baby sister. I also remember getting special treats from her—cheese and crackers. That is how I think of Pam—being gentle and kind and taking care of others.

From Rick:

I recently was asked to give my personal testimony to a church congregation. I once again shared how the Lord made himself known to me as a fifteen-year-old boy while I spent the summer with family members in Alaska. The Kaniuts were very gracious to ask me to live with them for the summer. I was a young boy with an unstable family background. I was very insecure and immature; however, they took me in. I remember that it was Pam who first began to talk to me about spiritual matters. I remember having discussions with her for the first time in my life asking myself questions about my eternal destiny. Larry had a tremendous impact on my life as well because he modeled Christianity for me as a man. But it was Pam who first questioned me and caused me to think. When I think of Pam, I remember someone who cared about my spiritual condition. The Lord truly used her in my life to bring me to the point of accepting Christ, and it was this decision that changed my life as a boy and as a man.

God bless you both. We love you and think of you often.

Beth and Rick

Alison Bjornseth Oct. 7, 2016

Larry - I don't have a specific memory of Pam, just a general memory of how sweet she is and how much my brother Eugene, loves you both. I remember reading your first Bear tales book and reading about Pam in there and thinking how cool and level headed she was. I know it isn't much, but I remember you both fondly. And I know that you both have provided love and support to my brother, when he needed it most.

Christopher Alexander Snyder

You and your family have always been very close to my heart. I may overflow you with pictures, but disregard those you do not want to use. I have many fond memories of my youth. The movie nights with the projector were some of the best. You and your family are all good people and I will always love all of you. I thank you, for above all you have been an incredible role model for how to live my life. And Pam has as well. Your family and the others have made my life in a way that my own family could not. And memories are gold. You have gone above and beyond, please know I learned from this.

Cindy Hamman, February 10, 1996 letter

We as horsewomen talk of a horse that has gentle eyes, but what about that of a woman? Through the eyes of the young she is very beautiful with her flowing blonde hair and petite figure, but what stands out the most is her utmost inspiration to me. I feel free to express my feelings of thankfulness not to mention her desires of gratitude in her day to day living with God as her Guide.

Though we may all work from day to day, not everyone sees this magnificent housewife behind her smile when she is indoors and may be hurting. She's very thoughtful and creative.

She and I have baked cookies together and I look forward to meeting her again. Could anyone here love so great as our lovely friend Pam, who also reaches out with a tender heart to all of God's creatures as well as everyone she meets? Only God knows.

What lies locked away in the secrets of Pam's heart? All those who know her can only tell of her treasures of compassion, and why she listens…she's a friend.

From a friend, Cindy Hamman

P.S. (from Cindy's mother)

To me, Pam must be an angel in disguise, taking Cindy under her wings when she needed a friend. She could never say anything negative about anyone, which is truly a gift from God. The cookouts were an extension of their love and graciousness.

Carol

Leslie L. Baldwin Jr., February 12, 1996 letter

The kind caring Heart of an Angel Friend

I come now to honor a loving lady. I was about 17-years-old when God moved me from a small town in Oklahoma to summer work with my uncle in Alaska. I was young, scared, new big changes going on. Then my uncle introduced me to a very special family, the Kaniuts. I was helped, and kindly treated by all. Pam Kaniut was ill the first time I met her. But a kind warm voice, with a smile of peace to others and welcome. I was invited to supper.

Pam looked pale and weak, but she cooked, cleaned, and talked wisdom, and never complained. Always showing strength of heart, love of her family, and love of God's animals. One summer I spent the night with the Kaniuts. The next morning I went to the table and Pam said, "Come and see this beautiful site." It was a mom moose with her calf in their yard.

Pam taught me by just being herself. "You can smile in pain." Your voice can display your loving heart. God's beauty can overshadow any troubles or pain. Loving others, and helping others is a better life. Life is hard for teens. Pam has given me a real look at God's love for others and a teacher of strength and wisdom.

There are so many great things about Pam I could make a book and others probably would not believe it's true. God's word says it best (Proverbs 31:25-31): "Strength and honor are her clothing; and she shall rejoice in time to come. She openeth her mouth with wisdom; and in her tongue is the law of kindness. She doeth well to the ways of her household; and eateth not the bread of idleness. Her children rise up and call her blessed; her husband also and he praiseth her. Many daughters have done virtuously, but thou excellest them all. Favor is deceitful and beauty is vain; but a woman that feareth the Lord, she shall be praised. Give her of the fruit of her hands; and let her own works praise her in the gates."

Larry, I really enjoyed being around your family. I know I was sent to learn from your lives

In closing, Pam should know that she did God's work here on earth. Others testify also of her special spirit. Pam, I wish you peace of spirit in times of trouble and kindness and love returned to you be tenfold. Bless you.

Julie Chase, April 24, 1990 note

Dear Beloved Mrs. Kaniut,

I love you and miss your fellowship! Forgive me for not writing or calling. Please don't think I've forgotten or avoided you because I haven't. I think of you and your serving spirit often. For I always feel refreshed after being with you, talking with you or reading a card or letter from you. I do notice every time you lift me up and encourage me by saying, "I've been thinking about you." Please continue to let Christ's light (or His love) shine through you, that is why so many people are drawn to you and never forget you. Everyone needs His love. I do hope that one day soon we could get together again. I love you, Mrs. Kaniut. Keep the faith.

In His love, Julie

Naedene Maslen Duran, facebook post May 17, 2016

I have such fond memories of Pam and her hospitality when we came to Alaska to visit. I was younger of course. Pam was so hospitable when we came. I remember riding in your car going to Flat Top to climb. Pam made some of the best sandwiches, I remember telling her that. It's been many years since Alaska, who knew food would be so memorable.

James Buchanon, April 13, 2016

During the FCA days, she was always a gracious host to a bunch of rowdy teenagers. Loved the cookies made with honey instead of sugar!

Ages between 15 and 18 years-old. Usually after a sledding day, or wood cutting party.

Michele Gibbens Otten Yes! I was there during the FCA days... heck, at the time I wasn't even an athlete or a Christian! But I sure enjoyed spending time in your home after sledding. I knew Larry as my English teacher and FCA sponsor, as well as at church. As uncouth (lol) as he was, Pam was completely the opposite! A calm, gentle, humble and sweet woman who would open her home even during a time when she physically wasn't feeling well. Pam, you modeled being a Proverbs 31 woman to me before I even knew what that meant! Thank you for influencing my life!

I now am the mom of a 23yo daughter and an 18yo son. I am a member of leadership in a bible study of over 200 women and 90 children! I also shepherd moms in my church.

Thank you Larry Kaniut and Pam for modeling Christ to me!

Jennifer Hughes Silverdale email May 16, 2016

Hello Mr. Kaniut!

I'm so happy to have heard from you about writing something for Pam. I think on your family often, and it settles my heart when hectic things are happening all around me. We lost my dad to pancreatic cancer in March, and Eric and I have spent a lot of time this spring reminiscing about our time in Alaska and great memories of your family. Please send my love to Ginger and Jill and their families...if possible, I'd love to get their addresses to send them a letter! Peace to you and Pam!

Love,

Jenny (of the Don-and-Rita-clan)

So here is my homage to a wonderful woman who blesses us all: My memories of "Mrs. Kaniut," whom I was compelled to call her out of respect and duty, but she was always ROSE in my brain, was a gentle and welcoming symbol of my youth in Anchorage. I believe I first thought of her as Rose due to Mr. Kaniut's loving references to her with this title, and affirmed in my heart that the church directory had certainly gotten her name incorrect, as Rose was far more suitable a name for her given the gentile woman I came to know.

Rose had bestowed on me two amazing, princess-haired daughters, Ginger and Jill, ideally spaced so that I was placed perfectly in between their ages and could enjoy both of them in play and at church gatherings. In my heart, I knew she had purposely done this just for me. I met Rose first at Oceanview Community Church through daughter Ginger, but I remember her most by the hearth at her home. Rose would be collected with a blanket on her lap in a chair by the hearth, usually reading when the raucous of children and tag-alongs would enter the house. I would, as many of us, be in tow by children or Mr. Kaniut, returning from church or school, ready to hang around, visit the horses, partake in a meal, or simply sit and chat. It was an easy thing to become an unofficial member of the Kaniut family, we followed the warm nature of the Kaniut clan back to their home, much like the Pied Piper from Hamelin, where we broke bread together and the afternoons would melt into late evenings of shared laughter and stories. Her daughters were much like Rose in nature and humor, and I found their genuine disposition both unusual and comforting.

Often I remember using the excuse to my mother, "The girls really need help mucking out the stalls today, so I need to go back with Ginger and Jill to help them get it all cleaned up." This usually worked, and even though the girls had completed this chore much earlier in the morning, I would be set for spending the rest of the day with their amazing family, trying to glean from them the meaning of the universe. It was just a relaxing place to be yourself in, and Rose made it a refuge for all.

If given the task of reiterating conversations with Rose, I can most remember her speaking the word of God to me in references to my teenage angst, trying to help quell the stress and pain of events which are most painful to teenagers. Rose was enormously patient and welcoming. I used to ponder how this lady remained so calm and collected with thunderous herds running throughout the house on numerous occasions. But she would pull one of us aside as we clamored past the hearth and into the kitchen and we would sit and tell her about our day and share our adventures. Rose could have taught a workshop on how to listen to others. Sometimes I thought I would talk her ears off, and she would let me go until I felt I'd emptied my soul to her. Upon completion of my verbal release, Rose had the most profound observations and would tie her thought to a Biblical verse or quote, which always drove the course of the conversation back to God. She had the wisdom of Methuselah and the patience of Job.

Now that I've taken on more of Rose's roles, becoming a wife and mother, I've noticed that many of my habits have been fashioned after my time spent at her home. She influenced how I prioritize things: I spend time being with people more than the unimportant housekeeping; we use the stairs for eventual transport of goods; I try to listen more than I speak; and, my family loves to do wonderfully random activities reflecting the joy we have for each other and the gift of life God has given us.

Kyle James April 25, 2016

Well I know for Marshall and I. Pam will always and forever be remembered in my heart at Christmas. I believe for Pam Christmas was the time to celebrate with friends and family and most importantly her love for God. And she did just that. She made a broken sad tree in the back yard into a gorgeous Christmas tree. It's totally like her to take something that had been seen as a sad broken tree or even a burden to have to be removed from the back yard, but to then decide to place it in her home and hang these beautiful family decorations. Also love how she convinced you to move into the house! And lovely you went along with this idea. The sweet treats she would make for Marshall and I every time we visited was just amazing. Every time I see white chocolate pretzels I see Pam in her kitchen making the sweet treats.

Many nights I watched as a child Pam talking to my mother at the kitchen table next to a burning fire while sipping tea and honey. I would listen to Pam giving my mother loving advice, sharing recipes and always offering Marshall and I anything we needed.

As an adult Pam explained the importance of introducing my son to God. I was really unsure as how to do this as my family wasn't big church goers. Pam had all the answers and for this I will always be thankful for.

Love Kyle

April Tincher Kaufman, May 1, 2016 facebook post

You both are very special to me. It was difficult for me to keep it focused on one of you while writing. You are a lovely couple serving Christ our Lord with beauty, grace and amazing unity.

In my recent reading of the Bible, my heart reads Jesus words, "Here's the lesson: Use your worldly resources to benefit others and make friends. Then, when your earthly possessions are gone, they will welcome you to an eternal home." The Book of Luke 16:9 My dear friend Pamela, you have learned Jesus' lesson well. You've shown me in your mild-tempered way how to take in a stranger (me) and treat her kindly, as one of you own. Be your treasures the offering of a warm room to rest in overnight, a freshly prepared (g/f) meal, or the patient ear of a genuine listener, you are intentional towards the benefiting of others and making them into friends.

I'm not certain which one of us will enter into heaven's gates first. But if I arrive first, it will be a special honor to me to be counted among your friends, your loved ones, and yes Jesus, to welcome you to your eternal home. And, if I may be transparent, the Lord knows the level of joy it is for me to hang out with a family that has just enough quirkiness to help me feel at home and even celebrate Easter together.

Honestly, I struggle at times with feeling truly at home in another home other than my own. And I sometimes wonder if am I the only one who at first feels a little insecure within myself being casual family company to the admired Larry Kaniut, popular Alaskan author and a favorite English teacher and legend to my Uncle Tom, who is also a former student?

And yet, Pamela, your relentless efforts to welcome me in to share life together with your whole family is amazing. Such grace, such kindness. Feels like Jesus himself loving me. You are a woman of courage, willing to trust the Lord Jesus in uncertain circumstances. Your life story exemplifies His faithfulness to you day by day. Witnesses like myself are encouraged by such exchanges of grace and beauty as the Holy One forms you, His child, more and more into His image. Only this kind of woman could continually grow in her giftedness as help-meet to her Christ-honoring husband who dotes on her and to her children who rise up and call her blessed.

Thank you for meeting and greeting me into your lovely home, into your family, with a warm hug and sparkle in your eyes. The memories of our farewells on the front patio are reminders of my "welcome back anytime" invitations. I especially thank you for your prayers for me. You and Larry have a place to call home when you're on the Kenai. You are family to me.

Love, April

PS Maybe one day you will have a family nickname for me, too. I'd like to have one that has to do something with courage.

Jeff Kliewer, February 12, 2005 e-mail

There are three memories of Pam that stick in my mind. One funny, one thankful, and one blessing.

First the funny one. When Ben and I were living together, the Kaniut family came to visit us during the month of August, probably 1998. Well, it just so happened that we were experiencing a significant heat wave in southern California and to go with it, our air conditioner was broken I'll never forget the picture in my head of Pam laying on Ben's bed with her feet wrapped in wet paper towels. It was really hot that day!

Thankful. Pam let me pet, feed, ride Prince. A great experience for a California boy who hadn't had a lot of experiences with horses. In fact, Pam even let me experience what it was like to get thrown off of Prince in the back yard.

The Blessing. During both stays in Alaska, Pam asked me to come sit near the kitchen window so I could look out into the yard and appreciate all the beautiful colors, plants and blossoms. She knows them all by name. It was a great lesson that most of the time, you need to sit down, slow down and just take a look at the simple things you see every day to appreciate God and His beauty.

Dan Bylsma, 4/22/2016 email Pam Kaniut   2007

My encounters with Pam have always been positive with joy coursing the conversations and experiences. While entering church for worship one Sunday I was commended by Pam with this verbiage, "It's nice to see smiles of anticipation on your face when coming to church." My reply was cursory and thankful; yet I was wondering to myself how uplifting that she noticed!

December, 2014

While on a mission at Christmas time to personally visit and thank as many local donors to our ministry; I made my way to the Kaniut residence. Pam answered the door and Larry appeared from outdoors. I thanked them for contributions and left some small gifts and Pam noted how special some of these items would be for the Grandkids. Not leaving without a hosted grand tour of their home and precious ministry and family stories that furniture and décor brought into the conversations. It was thrilling to me admiring the heritage that the Grandkids which I had briefly come to know would be mentored and nurtured in God's Word. Examples of Christlikeness at Christmas time...displaying, 'The reason for the season'!

Al Smay, note Feb. 12, 2018
My fifty-two years of knowing Pam

I met Pam in 1966 through her husband Larry who was my high school coach and teacher. They kind of took me in as one of the family. Pam treats everyone she comes in contact with the same. I have never heard her say a negative thing about anyone—she always thinks the best about each person she has contact with.

I have enjoyed many good times with the Kaniuts: drives down the Alcan, many picnics at their place; meals; gift exchange at Christmas and birthdays. Always enjoy the thank you notes and letters from Pam keeping us informed of what's happening with all the Kaniut family.

When I think of Pam, the words "country woman" come to mind. Pam is a true servant of the Lord Jesus Christ.

Proverbs 31: 10-31 is describing Pam especially verse 18, "her lamp does not go out at night."

Pam is a faithful wife, mother, grandmother, daughter, sister and friend. As a true friend Pam has been with the Smay family through the good times and not so good times. The Smay family appreciates you very much. Thank you for all your prayers over the last 52 years.

Al Smay

Jaylin Skrukrud   Valentine's Day homemade card

LOVE ("o" is a ♥). Happy Valentine's Day! Hope you guys have a wonderful day. Love, Jaylin (our 11-year-old neighbor girl)

Church

Donna (and Chester) Meeks

Larry,

Pam has left many memories on my heart and touched our entire family! Early memory of Pam was her hair!! Early in our Friendship, our two children (1966) the kids were fascinated with the length of Pam's hair. Rodney asked one day where did Pam rest her hair??? Fall of 1966 Pam flew with me and our two kids to Portland for each of us to visit Family. We carried fish, jam and frozen berries in bags, our pockets as well as suitcase. It was a joy to meet so many of the Timmons Family at the airport. Little did I realized those Family members became our lifelong Friends! Pam did that!

We spent a lot of time together playing games, eating and sharing what we had! We worshiped and attended Church together. Pam made the cutest finger puppets for ME to give to our kids to keep them occupied during Church! Pam did that!

Pam always wrote special letters to us at all our many addresses! Very artistic addressed envelopes-Larry did that!

One picnic brings hot memories to our Friendship Memory! A certain tall man in our midst started a fire on wet tundra, slow start--until gas was added! Pam worked so hard passing tools, a good blanket, and instructions for the crew of 2 men to put the fire out! Pam did that! Oh yes, I took pictures till a tall man noticed!!!

We completed our Family, six days later Pam started her Family!! Pam and Larry did that!!

In all Pam's health journey, her good days, her down days, she always remained positive that strength was coming soon! In new strength, Pam was always writing or gathering items to share with others. Pam has been a strong witness of Jesus' constant Love for her and brought her through health issues that many of us never understood or would handle it like Pam did!

Pam's love and prayers for her Family and her Grandchildren are often share with me and I treasure those.

Mary Ruth Curtis E-mail: Sept. 19, 2016

I'm pleased to share some reflections on our "Precious Pam" for that is what she is to us. There are only a very few who fit that title, and she fits it perfectly. I think of other titles that can be attached to her that come to mind right away when I start remembering things about Pam Kaniut. First, she is a Godly woman if I have ever known one. Just think of these words as a description of Pam: "Who can find a virtuous and capable wife? She is worth more than precious rubies. Her husband can trust her, and she will greatly enrich his life. She will not hinder him but help him all her life."

Gary, Brad, and I talked about their remembrances of Pam (and you, of course, for you have always been a team) in our early days in Alaska. Gary remembered times when Pam would babysit all the children of the Kendall and Ertz families (that would have been 5 at the time) while the adults were out together (serving the Lord and His church! Right??). Brad recalled, without the least hesitation I might add, that Pam made times in the Kaniut home so memorable and so much fun with her unique way of entertaining children. Even in their small home, she would take a quilt or blanket and spread it out in the living room and make a tent. Oh, what an exciting place to hear stories, read, share fun times, and best of all, eat "American Tacos"! Okay, maybe they were actually just a piece of bread, rolled around cooked ground beef, with lettuce, tomatoes, grated cheese and a bit of catsup. But they were yummy!

You two were so patient with those children as they grew into teens and needed even more understanding, special attention, and spiritual guidance. Even now I can remember that special little twinkle in Pam's eyes and the sly smile that seemed to come on her face when hearing about one of the inevitable escapades of those "youngsters" that meant she understood and loved them just the same.

Thank you, for helping our two sons enjoy church, being with Christians, and seeing Christ lived out with human hands and feet in such an attractive way. Brad noted the special feeling of family created there, when so many were away from their own blood relations, the church family (of which you and Pam were so definitely a part) filled that kind of void distance had created. For Gary at least, he would say that the beginnings of his call to ministry actually started there, in the basement of that little church on Sixth Avenue in downtown Anchorage, Alaska. The relationships he had in that special group were an integral part of his idea of what ministry was all about. No wonder that he was willing to devote over 30 years to "Love God, Love People, and Live Out" in serving as a Pastor.

So, thank you, Pam Kaniut, for being an example of that "wife of noble character" I spoke of at the beginning. "She speaks with wisdom, and faithful instruction is on her tongue....Her children arise and call her blessed; her husband also, and he praises her.... Give her the reward she has earned, and let her works bring her praise...."

We love you,

Mary Ruth (Kendall) Curtis, with Gary and Brad Kendall (follow up…76th birthday card, January 2018): see Pam's cards (addressed to Pamela Diane Rose Kaniut)

Gary Kendall, Feb 4, 2018, FBook post

Larry, my best memories were coming over to your home to play with my brother and your kids. Pam was always so gracious and a wonderful host. I felt at home. I liked the fact that we could play outdoors and enjoy nature. She was sweet and kind to us as kids.

Brenda Bauer   **April 2, 2005 letter**

Dear Larry,

When I think of Pam I have an empty spot in my heart for the lack of time that I would have liked to have spent with her. I believe that for the two short years that I had the privilege (1967-969) of getting to know and spending time with Pam were some of the most memorable years of my life. I remember our talks on the telephone, our house to house visits, being with Pam the day she started labor with Ginger, sharing my first pregnancy with Pam and taking our son Andrew to visit the Kaniuts on his first outing when he was a week old. We shared several meals together, and we had the privilege of meeting Pam's parents which was very meaningful. Pam filled such a void in my life since Alaska was the first time I had ever really lived away from my Family. Bob and I remember so well spending our last night in Anchorage with the Kaniuts celebrating Ginger's first birthday. I remember our good-byes and of course tears.

I still consider Pam one of my closest friends even though we do not talk or communicate with each other much. I had the opportunity to see Pam for a couple of minutes in Anchorage when Bob and I were getting ready to board a bus for a cruise to celebrate our 30th anniversary. Even though our time was short I left feeling so happy that I got on once again see my friend and knowing that she was and will always be the same person I got to know so well in the late sixties.

Pam, you are the best of people, best of friends, a wonderful Christian lady who has a gentleness about her like no one else. You have a smile and a laugh that I will always remember, and a devotion to your God, husband, children and grandchildren like no other. I consider myself so lucky to be able to call Pam Kaniut my friend and when I grow up I would love to be just like her!

Sincerely,
Brenda Y. Bauer

Chuck and Norma Fuller   **4/21/2016**

A long trip down Memory Lane resulted in our remembering

Pam as a woman with some powerful Godly characteristics: graciousness, kindness, and gentleness. We are so honored to be asked to share in this special project. Thank you.

Chuck & Norma

Wes and Ione Steele   **June 4, 1996 letter**

Dear Larry,

Ione and I are friends of Pam. We have known her for several years. We have been impressed with her ability to be cheerful and helpful while combating the health challenges in her life not to mention the challenge of marriage and raising a family. We agree with you. She is a sweetheart!

Your Alaskan friends,
Wes and Ione Steele

La Vonne Ertz   **December 2014** (church friend from 1971 to whom Pam sent flowers acknowledging La Vonne's illness)

Dear Pam,

Thank you so much for these spectacular flowers!! When I opened the door, I was "blasted" with a glorious smell! I didn't know flowers had that much! They are gorgeous! Pink and white day lilies, peach and pink colored roses and tall white and pink stems with lots of blossoms—they are wonderful! Thank you! I love em!

I remember coming to your house on days when you had so much pain you thought you were dying then—and so weak you could barely stand. And I wanted to help you: sweep your floor or do dishes or something—but you wouldn't let me. You always insisted that we just have a cup of tea and "visit." But then you always took me out to the porch to see your flowers, look at the geese, see the horse or the raspberries. I left refreshed and invigorated and you went back to your pain!

It has never seemed fair that you get all the pain and all of us get all the blessing! You have always been thankful, grateful for all God has done for you—you have been the ultimate inspiration for everyone who knows you! I can't imagine that anyone you know

43

has a better example in their whole life than you. No one who has met you can stand at the Judgment and tell God, "I just didn't know what a Christian was supposed to be like" as an excuse.

I can't imagine why God has seemingly ignored the many fervent prayers for your healing from hundreds of your friends—unless it's to prove to all of us that it is possible to endure extreme pain and agony with grace and peace and love and gratitude! (so we need to quit whining about our pitiful tiny trials!) Thank you for being faithful!! We love you and Larry.

Ralph and La Vonne

Karen Kendall,   **September 20, 2006**

(see input below from Karen—ten years later to the day)

It is said that in one's lifetime, if you have two or three true friends, you have been blessed. I consider myself blessed because I have been able to call Pam my friend.

There are so many wonderful things that can be said for Pam. However, Mother Teresa said something that I feel is so appropriate when it comes to explaining how I perceive her. She said, "It is not necessary to do great things, only small things with great love." Pam epitomizes that philosophy. She is constantly doing small things with great love for those who are lucky enough to know her.

Over the years there have been too many to name, but my family and I have been the recipients of countless special handmade cards, gifts of cookies and breads, recipes thoughtfully written, newspaper articles cut out and sent, goodie baskets "for the road", fabulous dinners and a constant awareness of one's needs. All of these are lovingly garnished with flowers from her garden and decorations to make sure you know she thinks you are special. She has the unique ability to make one feel appreciated and loved.

Another attribute of Pam's is her ability to see and appreciate the wonders of this world God created. I think because of so many days, weeks, months where she was unable to get out and run like the rest of us, she developed an appreciation for the beauty around her that we take so much for granted. She is constantly expressing thanks to

God for these things and it then helps one to see them too.

Also, Pam rarely meets a stranger but in her kind way she easily draws people to her.

In I Corinthians 13, Paul's chapter on love we can find Pam in every verse. I am so thankful I can call her "friend."

Karen Kendall   **9/20/2006**

Updated/letter received August 8, 2016

My mother loves and appreciates your letters and cards. What a wonderful ministry you have, Pam. A true blessing and she thinks you are the sweetest person in the world. I've known that for years and feel so blessed to be able to call you "friend."

Karen Kendall   **email Sept. 20, 2016**

My first recollection of Pam was in the spring of 1970. I had gone to a Women of the Church of God meeting and Pam had done the decorating. It was the first time I remember talking to her and I remember thinking how talented she was. Little did I know how blessed I would be by knowing her.

Many years have passed and my love, appreciation and respect for Pam has only grown. Despite having had long term health problems, she began a ministry where she sends letters and cards to some very lucky elderly people. On a regular basis she writes to them and sends cute, fun letters to cheer them and make them feel special. These are not just run of the mill letters and cards. She always does her best to make them interesting with pictures, decorations on the envelopes, colored stationery and anything else she can think of to make the person feel loved and treasured. The reason I know this is because my Mother is one of the people she writes to. I am fortunate because they are passed on to me and are enjoyed a second time. It is a unique and wonderful gift to these older people who may have no one who really cares or communicates with them.

Pam's dedication and determination to follow through on this is literally amazing. Despite her health issues, she makes sure that her letters go out without fail. I know how difficult it is for her at times and yet she is so disciplined that she just perseveres and gets it done. It is truly an act of love and compassion for others that drives her. She is constantly doing for others and when she gives a gift, you can be sure it is made with the utmost love and care.

Over the years I have noticed and benefitted from Pam's appreciation for beauty in so many places that most people overlook or just don't notice. I think in part because of the fact that she has been housebound at times, she has learned to appreciate the small things and see the beauty in them. Everything from the tiniest little plant sticking its head out of the snow in the spring, to the pink clouds floating overhead, birds getting hair off Prince's back (her horse) for their nests and the wonders of life in her yard and garden have always been sources of enjoyment for her. And, of course, she never tires ot the beauty and grandeur of Alaska. I think her ability to find beauty in small things and her love of people are traits that have made her the person that she is…one of the most Christ-like women I have ever known.

My life has been so blessed by her friendship. Time and circumstance have changed things a bit, but I still consider Pam to be my best friend. I know many people feel this way about her. She is one of the dearest friends a person would be fortunate enough to have. She sent me a card years ago that had the inscription on it saying "When we get to heaven, I hope my mansion is next to yours." I am looking forward to that.

With love always, Karen

Pastor Steve McCoy   **February 26, 1996 letter**

Hi, Pam

When I first met you, you were sweet, quiet, positive and reassuring. When you got really sick, you remained that way. Through trial, pressure, personal struggles and all sorts of unfair challenges you never wavered. I'm sure nothing has changed.

Pam, you are a true Christian and a champion. You've done the best you could to make a home, you've some GREAT CHILDREN, and you've set an example with your life of the power of Christ working in a person.

God bless you, Pam. Keep fighting the good fight. In case you haven't noticed…you're winning!

Pastor Steve McCoy

Quency Light   May 5, 1996 letter

Dear Larry,

When I think of Pam, I picture her as the kind of mom I want to be. As a mom, I'm sure there were (are) things Pam wanted to do for your children, but she wasn't physically able to. Her prayers for your children and the fact that they were more independent and helpful (around the house) at an early age contributed to the wonderful character of your adult children.

Pam is the kind of Godly woman I would like to be.

A friend,
Quency Light

Ronni Woolrich   April 15, 1996 letter

Larry,

It's almost impossible to express adequately what I feel about Pam. She is as you say—really an angel and a saint.

I first met Pam in (I think) the late '70s or early 80's through our mutual church. In 1981 I came down with a dreadful, incurable disease. At that point in my life I was totally unable to care for myself and spent over a year in a wheelchair that I couldn't push. Meanwhile, my small children ages 4 and 5 and husband had to do everything. I was in unbelievable pain and totally bedbound. My knees got bloody from crawling to the bathroom.

It was about this time I met Pam. I was unable to go anywhere, so we talked constantly on the phone. She, too, was battling terrible health problems yet she could reach out to me and bring me such comfort. Finally I was diagnosed with the disease Reflex Sympathetic Dystrophy. Later, when I read the literature, I knew I wasn't crazy because it is known to be "more painful than cancer—

probably one of the worst types of pain known to man." It has a high suicide rate, and most people would amputate the affected limbs if it would do any good.

I was understandably depressed and in deep despair. It is the only time in my life I wanted to die. What kept me alive was my faith, my family, and Pam. She was an endless source of mental "strength" to me. In her quiet, unassuming, modest way, she lifted me up every time I spoke with her. I don't know what I ever would have done without this dear friend to talk to. She gave me courage, renewed my faith, and helped me face the world. She did this while she herself was suffering terribly.

Meanwhile, I was sent to the University of Washington Hospital in Seattle. After being there three months and having eight surgeries on my spine, I came home. My battle had just begun. I had to learn to walk again. It was five years of agony and mostly being in bed.

We lost our home, all of our possessions, and eventually our father/husband. But I didn't lose Pam. She was always there—my source of inner strength.

I took my two wonderful girls to Washington state to be near medical care. Slowly my pain got less although I will always have this disease.

Till this day, though Pam and I are separated by thousands of miles, I still consider her my dearest friend. I feel she is God's gift to me—my own guardian angel. I know she will always "be there" for me, as I am for her. She has touched my life in a way no one else has—she truly is the embodiment of Jesus' teaching in Matthew where he says, "anything in my name."

In His care, Ronni

And a July 1998 Thank you card from Ronni:

Hi Pam, There's not a time that I don't thank God for you! Your friendship sustains me so often I just wish I could pick up the phone and call you every day. Some time I'll call you and we'll talk. Thanks so much for the fragrance. It is lovely!

Lorraine O'Neal   **March 30, 2005 e-mail**

Hi Larry Kaniut,

I have fond memories of Pam. She is one of the sweetest and most cheerful women I've ever had the pleasure to meet. I love her gentle spirit and happy outlook on life even in the midst of great physical challenges. I appreciate her openness and kindness toward guests in your home. Pam makes it a welcome place for all.

I did not have opportunity to spend very much time visiting, and it has been quite a few years but I will always remember the love and warmth of the Kanuit home. It is obvious that you've both done a good job of teaching your children by example how to live. The blessings of the Lord are upon you and the work of your hands.

It's good to see the love and support you both have for one another. In fact, just thinking of the precious times of fellowship we had in the past makes me want to come over and visit. I may surprise you one of these days! It would be good to catch up and person and share some tea. Bless you Pam and Larry!

Well bless you
Lorraine

Alice Noble   April 2, 2005 letter

Dear Larry,

I am glad to say a few things about one of the greatest Christian women I have known in my lifetime. I will always remember Pam and her quiet countenance.

Mainly I remember the wild rice that she gave me one Christmas. What a pleasant surprise, a ten-pound bag of rice. She told me why she was giving it to me. I looked very much undernourished at the time. But then, she was thinner than I. Still, I thought, "how very observant." How many people would think to do this and in this special way? There was a list of recipes for cooking it, too. Also she had compiled a list of nutritional facts, which she emphasized as important. How could I ever forget?

I appreciate those people with special insights and I will always remember her, because she prayed for this thin and troubled woman

49

and gave me a gift that I have never forgotten. Of course it wasn't the gift so much as the thought that she cared about me.

When I most needed her prayers she prayed for me. She listened. The first time I was in her home she showed me around then we sat in front of that fireplace and talked and prayed. She prayed with me while she lay by the fireplace on a pallet, on one of the days she felt her strength fade.

I remember a particular sweet demeanor. I believe it is God's presence in her that gave her the ability to see my needs. I believe that she "lives as a shining light" to those who know her.

I remember her kind and gentle voice and how soothing it was to my soul when I was most troubled. I remember feeling a loss in my life when we were not longer close friends. You had by then moved to Alabama for a couple of years and this was when we lost contact. I will always believe she has a close walk with the Lord and never judges people.

To sum this all up I loved her then and I love her now.

P.S. My love to you, Pam and family.

Rita Hughes   May 9, 2016 email

Hi Larry,

It was good to hear from you in April and I'm so glad that you are completing your book about your sweet wife, Pam. That word really embodies who she is and how I have always remembered Pam! The nicknames that you included were a surprise to me...I'd never heard her called by any of those, but they were cute. During the 12 years that our family lived in Anchorage and were active at Oceanview, your family really stands out in my mind. Both you and Pam have been remarkable parents (and probably grandparents several times over by now). You provided your kids with a remarkably creative environment and fostered their faith in Christ always. You were hilarious, and always up for some fun prank...I remember our family following your family's car on the way to church, when we were meeting at Service High, and we couldn't figure out why you were driving soooo slowly and then you sped up so fast at times. And then when we found out you were coasting all the way up and down those rolling hills that morning....well it was just the Kaniut way of having mischievous fun that morning. I always saw your family members as free spirits...with you at the helm, leading the way, and Pam as the ballast for your family...probably keeping you even through it all. What a great match you two have been together, with Christ at the center of your lives! I look forward to reading your book when it's published. I know it will be wonderful.

I remember our years in Alaska as 12 of the happiest and most productive years of our lives together. Being a part of Oceanview made a life-changing difference in our lives and in our children's lives. Knowing the Kaniut family...our kids growing up together there....well you were a blessing...no, a joyful tonic to our lives. You showed us how to live joyfully...that spunky spirit of yours must have made some scratch their heads at times. Pam was certainly the heart of your home! We could never forget you or your family!

Love to you and your whole family, in Christ,
Rita

Bonnie Hemry   Nov. 26, 2016 email

I met Pam Kaniut about 13 years ago when my daughter married her son. At first our relationship was that of in-laws to our children, but in the years since then, it has become much more than that. Pam, and her husband, Larry, have become some of my best friends. Our relationship has grown out of not only family ties but our love of the Lord as Christians. As I think of the reason this has happened, I know it is because of the unconditional love I have received from them. They are ever-welcoming, ever-caring, non-judging, eager to affirm others and share their own lives.

When I think of Pam, qualities that come to mind are gracious, loving, serving, caring, self-effacing. Her home is her castle and she opens the doors to all who come, caring for them with her servant heart. Seated around the table next to the fire, guests are served special treats, closely attended by Pam, while Larry relates stories of times past. The warmth of the atmosphere and fellowship displaces any self-consciousness and concerns for propriety, replacing them with heart-felt, mutual sharing. I, along with my grandchildren Joseph and Christine, have experienced many good times with Pam and Larry—campfire and roasted hot dogs in winter, a stroll through their garden, square dancing on their back porch, riding beloved Prince, to name a few. More than any other person I know, Pam represents the heart and hands of Jesus to all those He brings to her. I, and my grandchildren, have been blessed to be a part of this group.

Bonnie

Gene and Jeannie Wallace   letter (c. 1996)

Jeannie and I have known Pam and Larry for over 20 years. Whenever anyone meets them one is immediately struck with the impression that they now know someone special, even unique. That was my impression years ago, it has proven out and intensified in the ensuing years. A letter or conversation with them is always a special occasion.

There is one overriding feature that strikes you about Pam and Larry—family. Nothing else is more important nor elemental in their lives. The product of their efforts is evident today in the lives of a strong family, everyone including in-laws and out-laws, committed to the cause of Christ.

Each of us in the life process brings God given traits, skills and unique characteristics to our marriages and relationships with friends. Some better than others. One of the most valuable of these characteristics is courage. In my journey through life I discovered many who boast of it, many who play at it, but few who in the course of life live it. And live it to such an extent that God uses them as examples for the rest of us who boast of courage. Webster defines courage as the "ability to conquer fear or despair: Bravery, Valor", but I have had the privilege of seeing it in action and the joy of knowing it and having a close and loving relationship with two people who live courageous lives, one of those people is Pam

Kaniut.

I have watched thru the years a woman of courage seldom display a negative spirit even when very sick. In the face of a diagnosis of no hope for a cure, Pam never falters as her faith shines through—courage is shown. When a possible solution or cure is suggested she maintains a rock steady walk without becoming too hopeful yet hopeful, that takes courage. In today's world there are too few people who live by the courage of their convictions. Some day when I cross the Great Divide, I will not boast of anything, but I will thank God for the gift of Salvation, my wife, children and grandchildren and for placing many people in my path. I can also say that I knew a special woman who was my friend and who helped me see courage in action.

In Christ, Gene and Jeannie Wallace

Cliff Carrell   **May 4, 2016 e-mail**

I think of you all frequently and I cherish the memories of our hunting and fishing escapades during my 3 year stint in Alaska. You are a very lucky person to have such a caring devoted wife to share your life with. Pam is also a very lucky person to have you in her life. Even through her illness she was the epitome of the perfect hostess, always taking care of those around her before thinking of her own needs. You both helped me more than you will ever know during my lengthy recovery from my burn accident.

Thank you both for everything and I hope to get to see you sometime in the near future!

Love you all, Cliff

Louise Kucera   **February 7, 2005 letter**

Thinking of You, Pam…

Although we have seen one another only occasionally over the years, you remain a woman I look up to and have enjoyed knowing. Since we generally visited in your home, Tom and I had opportunities to see your home evolve from one level to an expanded two-level. As

Alaskans sometimes do, you and your family lived in one section as you built the rest of your home. Your home turned out so beautifully.

The first time I met you in 1976, I was impressed with your peaceful countenance, friendly smile, and the pure enjoyment you had in being a loving wife and mother…a model to all women. Your family enjoyed working together on various projects and enjoyed the horses stalled outside your backdoor.

I remember visiting with you at our home just before Tom died in 2002. Larry and Tom talked with one another at the dining table, discussing aircraft and Larry's dream to have one of his own. You and I talked while sitting on sofas looking out over the lake, chatting about our respective families and techniques being used to improve your health. It was a beautiful, sunny day!

I have never known you to be in good health, but you and your family continually work around your limitations in a wonderful way. You do what you can, they support you as they can, and your family interacts in a beautiful manner.

Pam, four things stand out when I think of you: 1) peaceful countenance, 2) living today, 3) working on projects destined to be completed tomorrow, 4) and most of all, modeling Christian values in all that you do.

You have been greatly blessed with a wonderful and supporting family…a husband, three children, and grandchildren. All walk in the Lord and are excited about the lives they have been given. Wonderful blessings, indeed.

May your life be continually surrounded with such goodness.
Louise Kucera

Debbie Yingling   thank you card Feb. 10, 2018
Dear Sweet Pam
Words can't say how very much all your wonderful letters/notes/ daily diaries have meant to me since moving from AK to PA! You are one-of-a-kind and the most awesome friend in the world. Your thoughtfulness and selflessness are continuous blessings to me.

Thank you for being you! And thank you for phone calls (I love catching up over the phone!). And the beautiful birthday card with flower $ enclosed. You are special to so many for the so many ways you bring cheer to lives (Jill had a good example).

May God richly bless every day of your life. He sure blessed my life with your friendship.

Love you and see you soon Debbie

FBook post Feb. 17, 2018

Hi, Larry. Hope this qualifies as an entry for your Pamela Rose project.

Dear Pam, Your friendship has been a huge blessing to me for many, many years!! Since moving to PA 17 years ago, your frequent letters, cards, gifts, flowers and short diaries (how you spend your days) have been constant day brighteners. You've always been a source of inspiration and kindness, as well as a reminder of the beautiful Alaska I left behind. You're such a gifted artist who, with words, paints pictures that warm my heart and refresh me with AK memoires. (The beauty of the envelopes are equally artistic, impressive and thoughtful!) You go above and beyond to bring cheer to my life—and many others as well. I cherish your friendship and thank God for crossing our paths. I fondly remember meeting you for the first time when I delivered to you a "shut in" gift box from Cornerstone Church, and for the majority of our visit you asked all about me and my family. You were so kind and caring and didn't want to talk about yourself, you were interested in learning about me and my family. Your selflessness was apparent that first visit. Your and Jill's visit to our home in PA was such fun (at least for Carl and me!!!!) and a great opportunity to see just how much you love ice cream!!! The laughs and day trips were tremendous fun. A repeat visit would be AMAZING!!!Please come back anytime and bring anyone!! I love you and appreciate you immensely!!! P.S. Carl really enjoyed your and Jill's visit too)

Teachers and Colleagues

John and Delores Lindeman   **February 14, 1996 letter**

Our hearts rejoice when we recall the pleasant memories of our brief encounters with Pam Kaniut since 1966 when we met in Newberg, Oregon. Larry and Pam broke trail moving to Alaska in the summer of 1966 and we were welcomed at their new home in Anchorage when our caravan of three vans arrived in Anchorage that summer as tourists, and they accompanied us down the Kenai Peninsula as far as the Russian River where they introduced us to "combat fishing" and Larry snagged a seagull in the process. We cooked up fresh salmon on the campfire that night and with Alaska stories flowing, it was a grand evening. In 1968 we moved to Ninilchik, Alaska, and with John and Larry both coaching wrestling, we touched base many more times over the next years. Pam and Delores were full time moms so we shared our children and many common interests over the years, our last get together here at our farm in Ninilchik during the summer of 1994, where we did a lot of catching up, and again we rejoiced in the friendship we all shared. Under every circumstance during these 30 years Pam has been smiling, joyful and upbeat, in spite of the obstacles of her sickness. Her life is a testimony of one who serves a living God, and we have observed the clarity and care with which she loves others, which speaks with vitality of the great gift of life she has been to all she comes in contact with. Thanks, Pam for touching our lives.

Delores and John Lindeman

Peggy Ames Merritt   **February 20, 1996 letter**

Dear Larry,

It is so evident how blessed you are with the relationships in your family. And it's certainly not a one-way street. They're blessed too! No doubt they know that; I'm sure Pam does.

When I called last, visited briefly with Pam, and she said "Well, I wish my sweet husband were here. I know he'd like to talk with you," it just made me feel so good. I've never known Pam, even when she wasn't feeling well, to speak in other than a kind, loving manner in her well-modulated voice. It's so uncomfortable being around couples who don't seem to like each other or who are always playing the "oneupsmanship" game, but that has never been the case with you two. I am often reminded though of a remark Mark made when he was just a kid. We hadn't known you long when he said of Pam, "She scares me." When I asked what on earth he meant, he said, "Well, she's just so perfect."

Jean Kurtz   **February 20, 1996 letter**

Father Brian of the Priests of the Sacred Heart, repeats this story told to him by a Chinese missionary:

A little boy asked his grandfather, "What is hell like?" The grandfather answered, "Hell is like this. There is a sumptuous banquet table full of delightful food. The people, however, are cursing and swearing. Their chopsticks are too long for them to feed themselves."

The boy then asked, "What is heaven like?" The grandfather answered, "there is a banquet table just the same, but instead of cursing, there is joy and singing and dancing. The only difference is that in heaven, the people feed each other with those long chopsticks."

Larry and Pam shared that same way with me on a miserable day. One day, years ago, I was more than usually blue so I called the

Kaniuts and invited myself over. As luck would have it, I arrived at dinner time. "No problem," Pam said, as she cheerfully stretched the meal. I was quickly recovering from the blues as the whole family talked, joked and welcomed me. After dinner, I offered to do the dishes, and Pam graciously declined my offer. It was an expression of Christian hospitality which I'll never forget.

When the Brothers asked St. Francis, "Who is the best preacher?" St. Francis thought a minute and then replied, "the best preacher is Brother Example."

Thanks and cheers to Pam and Larry, too.

Jean Kurtz, Friend (Larry's Dimond High teaching colleague)

P.S. from Jean
I met Pam only a few times, and she's priceless.

Lynn Romagoux   February 27, 1996 letter

Hello, Good Friend,

Pam's physical weaknesses have allowed her to develop her personal strengths and beliefs in those around her. Donna and I observed and have interacted with many of her brightest accomplishments: her home, her husband, and her magnificent children. Pam's care and giving, her love of others are part of our acceptance into your Alaskan family when we were invited into your home while living in our camper on your property while our new home was being completed. A little later in time Pam, you provided strength for Donna when your husband spent an unexpected night, unprepared on a mountainside with me. Throughout our close relationship we have always prayed for an answer to the disease. But we've also loved the strong, quiet, giving Pam.

Cal Pappas   February 12, 1996 letter

Bravo on your choice for this book—it's well deserved.

It was nice how Pam opened her (your) home to me after our trip in '85—also before, when I stored my stuff with you.

I've never heard Pam speak ill of anyone—even if they deserved it. Without question, she is the most kind and giving person I've met. The New Testament shows the works of love (patience, longsuffering, not jealous, etc.) which are personified in your wife. I've never seen her without her patented smile and I know she would do anything for anyone.

Good luck with your book. I know if I was lucky enough in the past to find a woman like Pam, I'd be happily married today. Who knows—maybe I will!

Best to you, Pappas

$\mathcal{N}eighbors$

Gordy and Karon Best   **April 4, 2005 letter**

Dear Larry:

So very sorry to hear of Pam's continuing battle for better health. It seems the poor woman has had more than her share. We often think of you folks and really enjoyed our brief visit a couple of years ago. We regretted leaving home and friends back in 1973 but duty called.

Karon and I have read and re-read your newsy letter and are grateful you remembered us. Please convey our sincere and heartfelt hope for quick solutions to these ongoing health issues.

Your former neighbors and life long friends, Gordy and Karon

Larry,   **email from Sonny and Carole Miller 4/25/2016**

Nice to hear from you and yes you will see us soon, sometime in June. Below I am writing a comment about Pam that both Sonny and I said at the same time, so it must be true.

When our family thinks of Pam our first thought was always "safe house". Because Pam was home almost all of the time both Nicole and Aaron knew growing up if ever there was a problem, and Sonny and I weren't home, they could always go across the street and be safe until we returned home. Pam would never turn away a child who came to her door and that remains true to this day.

Vic and Vickie Baer,   **e-mail, April 14, 2018**

My Proverbs 31 Friend

Her lights burn late into the night. I could
see her outdoor light from our window and it
shown through our window. I referred to it as my night
light. Her hands are busy always delivering delicious
baked goods to neighbors and friends. You felt loved in her
home. Deeply loved! She will be greatly praised!

Forty-three years ago, my Dear Friend Pam who I now refer to as my Proverbs 31 Friend came into my life. Through all those by-gone years, it's been so very obvious that her Christian walk was indeed directed by our Creator! She was my neighbor and I think the entire neighborhood would agree that she became the "neighborhood Mom, Grandma and kindest to every child she came in contact with". She possessed the beautiful gift of hospitality! One particular day when our children would walk home from the bus, she invited our Lynette and Heidi in for an after-school snack. Homemade taco shells and all the toppings. They still talk about that feast thirty-five years later. Homemade donuts on Halloween and the feasts go on and on. Rain or shine, every May Day for forty plus years, we would find a beautiful bouquet hanging on our outdoor knob. My Mom spent several years in the Juneau Pioneer's Home and nearly every week, she would receive a beautiful letter from Pam (sometimes written at 4:00 am). These weren't just letters. Pam would decorate them with cut out pictures, stickers, etc. Loving on everyone. She is an Angel clothed in compassion, kindness and gentleness. Many times, I've thought "I want to be like Pam!" We love her and her family dearly!!

Vic and Vickie Baer

Pat Murphy   May 12, 2016 letter

We moved to Anchorage in 1976 and were transferred out in 1983. During that time our daughters became best of friends—Pam Kaniut was always that strong friend always there, very communicative about the girls, constant in supporting the instillation of Christian values in these girls. This is why I trusted they were in good hands any time my girls were at the Kaniut house or with the Kaniut girls. My elder, Catherine, writes the following (she is now 47-years-old):

We were neighbors and friends from the 4th to the 8th grades— Pam is a very clear memory. She was a kind of second "mom." We spent a lot of time between homes—but Pam had a horse in the backyard and my sister and I, as all young girls, loved horses. I remember hot chocolate on the stove made from milk and powdered chocolate, hot cookies, sleeping in sleeping bag in the wonderful living room with the round table with chairs that fit underneath it. We dressed up as Geisha girls with Ginger for school. Pam had the best art projects to keep us occupied and we learned many paper and fiber and fabric crafts that way. She was always kind, no matter how irritating we were, as young girls can be irritating and have disagreements at times.

As Catherine's mom, I appreciated having Pam there for me and my daughters as for a long time I worked nights, then switched to 12 hour days. I remember a call from my younger daughter Charlene saying that they could not go to school since there was a moose in the road. I told them I was going to call Mrs. Kaniut and if she said there was a moose in the road, then they could not go on the road, but if Mrs. Kaniut said there was no moose in the road, they were going to school and I would call the school to be sure they were there. Needless to say, they went to school.

It is said "it takes a village to raise a child." Pam was always part of that village. When my younger daughter was dying, Pam, Ginger and Jill were there for me and for Charlene. This is truly God's work and living the Word. Even after Charlene was gone and I had to return to my home on the East Coast, Pam, Jill and Ginger were there for my grandson (Charlene's son was only 9 when he lost his mom). I cannot think of a more kind, loving, Christian woman who lives her faith more than Pam Kaniut. She will always have my eternal gratitude and be in my prayers.

Pat Murphy

In the ten years we've been neighbors with Pam, we have appreciated the little opportunities that have led to her smile and wave as we walk by, as well as the deeper times when we've stopped and caught up on life. We know our children have an extra eye on them while playing outside or we can always borrow a cup of sugar. We value Pam as a neighbor who cares.

> Marcus and Ingrid Reese

Tamie Hollingsworth

I met Pam Kaniut in 1970, adding on to their current home on Natrona, in Anchorage, AK. She was a plain-looking, simple, country gal. Of course, she was chatting with the women who would pop in, while their boyfriend or husband would be helping Larry with the addition. There was always a lot of "extra" help with high-school students wanting to feel a part of whatever was going on, and Pam always would be fixing snacks or drinks and making them feel special. Making others feel special is a signature mark of Pam's life...perhaps her mission in life itself.

In 1976 I graduated from high-school myself, and spent many summer nights at the Kaniut house playing Rook with Larry and Randy Terry. Pam always had something to eat- but nothing fancy. A small bowl of nuts on the table, a single muffin with jam, or perhaps some fresh-picked berries. Just a handful to make you feel special, but not enough to fill you up! At college, Pam would send care packages to ALL the kids who were former students of Larry's, and other family friends. I think she sent me chocolate chip cookies once. Always with a hand-written card...just to make you feel special. And I did. In 1979, both the Kaniut girls Ginger and Jill were flower girls in my wedding, and when I had babies, Pam would let the girls spend the night with me and help babysit because my husband was a commercial fisherman in the summer. One summer in 1985 I was either sick or afraid, but Pam invited me and the 3 kids to come spend the night.

Through-out the years, Pam and Larry would have a revolving

door at their house. Students who had graduated YEARS earlier refused to move on! They just kept coming back, to hear Larry's stories, and to catch Pam's attention, because, she always made them feel special. She was known during those 80's and 90's for her pies (and the homemade ice cream that often came, too). In the 2000's she was known for her chess pies (dates/nuts/raisin tarts), and, her hand dipped, pan-fried fresh clams! And when she invited you over for dinner, that might be the only thing on the menu- that, and incredible conversation focusing on YOU, and what you were doing. She made everyone feel special.

In 2015, my mother died. Pam brought beautiful single-serving pieces of melon to her. And, a single muffin, wrapped with a doily and tied with a ribbon. Perhaps a small piece of chocolate tucked in, to make her feel special. And, after she died, I had surgery on my leg. And, Pam and Larry brought cups of ice for icing my leg, and made me breakfast, and brought 2 muffins with a hand-written note. To make me feel loved, and special, and cared for. And in 2018 after my leg froze up and I had another surgery, they came again. Bringing a beautiful potted tulip plant, and offered to bring ice once more.

So the ingredient that Pam brings to the table is not expensive or hard to find. It is not lavish, nor does it require perfection to be appreciated. It is the gift of herself, her listening ear, and her selfless gift of putting others first. She embodies the golden rule of "treat others as you would have them treat you". She takes the time to use whatever resource she has, and make it beautiful. She turns a simple muffin into a special treat hidden by ribbons and colored boxes. She takes paper and scissors and helps a child create a barn or an exotic animal from their imagination. It takes time, and that is what she always is willing to give, to make each person feel special.

Pam, it is such an honor to have been your friend for 48 years, and your neighbor for 26yrs and counting! You are a very unique, special lady. Thank you for showing me how to love others, and how to wisely use the resources one has. You have shown by example, without instruction but with your words, how to love others and minister to the hurting. Your legacy is being carried on by your daughter Jill who has learned from the best. Blessing to you, dear Pam.

I love you,
Tamie

Others

Jody Garcia   **April 27, 1996 phone call**

She's a lover of life. Once in the winter of 1982 when I was discouraged, Pam told me how beautiful it was outside; and I realized I wasn't really appreciating life. Every time I see some heavy rain, beautiful snow and natural beauty, I think about Pam's snow and I am reminded that God is so good. I appreciate her because she is a lover of life and inspires others to love life too.

Virginia Snyder and Helen Partlett   **May 22, 1996 letter**

Dear Larry,

This is such a neat idea of yours. Also, it gives me an opportunity to write a long overdue letter expressing my gratitude—especially to Pam---for all of the many kindnesses you have done for me and my family in Anchorage. Take from it what you want (if anything) for your book.

I first met Pam in 1975 after the death of my daughter-in-law, Beth. Pam had been called many times by six-year-old Chris during the previous winter and spring to help with his sick mother. This went beyond mere neighborliness.

Next, at the time of the tragic death of my son's mother-in-law, Lorraine, I renewed your friendship. Pam, in spite of not being well, took Lorraine's sister, Helen, and me "under her wings" during the time we were there. Especially, she was the spirit directing the Christmas and New Year celebrations thinking of us and others who were away from home and our immediate families.

Lastly, Pam's friendship and continued support of my son, Carl, and grandson, Derek, over the past six years has been a great comfort to them both and to me.

Thank you, Pam from the bottom of my heart! Yours is the true Christian spirit at its very best.

Sincerely yours,
Virginia Snyder

I first heard about Pam from my sister, Warwick, who was her neighbor. She was a wonderful friend to Lorraine, and also to me when my sister was killed in a hit-run accident, and I came to Anchorage to stay with Lorraine's grandchildren. She helped so much with the children, and many other things during my two months' stay.

Pam is still being a wonderful neighbor and friend to Derek and Carol. To me she is the kind of person God meant for us all to be.

Sincerely,
Helen Partlett

Kay Shively

Wasilla former Thomson-Shore worker with our first self-published book

Although I've known Pam only briefly, I've found her to be an amazing woman. She welcomed me into her home, an unknown person, as if I were a friend she had known for years. Comfortable to be with is another way to describe her. I had ease in talking with her as if I had known her forever. She very obviously is devoted to her family, the kids and grandkids and appears to be the pivot point for the entire family. Pam is the heart of this family and I feel very honored to know her. I only wish we could find the time to get together as I'd love for her to meet my husband. Thank you for giving me a chance to voice my feelings...

Your friend in Wasilla,
Kay Shively

Sherry Merchant   **4/17/2016**

Pam is a wonderful person whom I've grown close to in the last few years. I love her to pieces and enjoy her company. Pam is true blue from heart and soul and I know that God has selected her as one of his angels on earth. We've had BBQs in the past and Pam brought her famous pies...yum...and always warm, just baked. Pam also brought me plants to put out because she knows I like gardening. I planted what she brought and they are doing so well and think they were christened by her angelic aurora. Where nothing else would grow, her plants she brought did! Pam is a warm and tender person and will always be close to my heart forever.

Janice Eckard   **4/19/2016**   **6:20 AM (14 hours ago)**

Hi Larry!

First of all, thank you for inviting me to share in such a personal, precious project!!Even though I have never met you or Pam in person, I feel as though I know you and could feel so at home around you both.

Whenever I called and Pam answered, I could not have asked for a sweeter response (especially from someone who had never met me. She was so genuinely excited to talk to me).

She has this way of making you feel as though you are part of her family and she cares about you and yours.

She always sends letters, (which takes so much time to write) even though she is extremely busy and sometimes doesn't feel well (although she rarely mentions that). There are people who I come in contact with in person, who don't make me feel as special as she does.

For the record, you BOTH are people that God has definitely put here for our blessings!!

Thanks again,

Janice

Please keep in touch!! We are still trying to plan a trip back to Alaska and hopefully soon!

(Update: Feb. 8, 2018) Hi Larry!

Great to hear from you! Thank you for allowing me to join in. One of the things that sticks out in my mind about Pam is that whenever we get to talk on the phone, which is not often enough, she sounds so excited and happy to hear from us in N.C.

She is so sweet and genuinely cares about what is going on in our lives. Even though we have never met in person, I feel as though I've known her for years. She is so proud of her family and her love of God comes through loud and clear. I feel so blessed to have gotten the chance to become her friend. I also love to receive letters in the mail from Alaska because I know it always contains something about what is going on in her life, plus she always asks about mine!!

Take care and can't wait to read the final product!

Pam writes Janice: **(March 2012)**

Howdy from our tiny farm, here on the edge of Anchorage.

We live in the foothills of the Chugach (choo-gatch) Mountains so we are very close for hiking and view the mountains from our home. About two miles west we grab the freeway (that didn't exist in 1970 when we bought our property and built our home) and go right into town or drive along Turnagain Arm with mountains to the left hugging the road (and Dall sheep coming down to the highway) or look north or south to view the Chugach and Kenai mountains. West from our house we view the Alaska Range, home of Mt. Mc Kinley, North America's tallest mountain (and the highest in the world if you consider it rises from flat land to its summit). How blessed we are.

Yesterday we had lunch with a lady who has lived in North Carolina and she spoke of NC's beauty also. We hope to be there in the next six months to see for ourselves.

It was 4 degrees this morning. The sun is sending bright shadows on the snow. One of the icicles hanging off the kitchen roof is nearly 6-feet in length...and snow is 3 to 5 feet deep around the yard.

Since Dec. 22 we've been gaining light. It's such a wonderful feeling for us. It's light by 7 AM and until nearly 9 PM. Then in June and July we have only a few hours of dusk in Anchorage. People visit others until midnight without thinking much about it. We have gardened at 11 PM.

Larry and I came here in 1966 for one year. But, God had other plans. Our children have loved the Alaska life. We've had great churches and schools and Larry may never have been asked to write a bear book if we hadn't been here. Then, more publishers asked him to write other books. Later we published our own books…and Larry is working on three these past few years, with more ideas if time permits. The books he is finishing up are about airplane flying stories in Alaska, another bear book and a Christian novel that takes place in the time of Jesus Christ.

Alaska is so large that weather, sunlight, etc. are different in each area. Anchorage is a big city with heavy traffic, big known stores, malls, etc. There are so many tiny villages; we don't know their names. Most of them are accessible only by plane or boat—we have something like less than 3,000 miles of highways in the state.

Janice said "thank yous" would be coming our way. Well, Tuesday they arrived but you were so very thoughtful to add pictures and gifts as well. We appreciate the thank yous from the children. It's easy to see the children are each unique. We didn't understand much about Alaska as we headed up the Alaska Highway so I can see why they'd have questions too.

Several of the children asked about our horse. He's a full size, white Appaloosa and Prince will be 31-years-old in April. His teeth aren't good enough to chew hay so twice a day we soak small, hard cubes of chopped-pressed alfalfa in water. It comes up the long Alaska Highway from Washington State. In late August his hair begins growing longer. If he has enough food, that food also helps to keep him warm. Prince likes being outdoors so stands out in the rain, snow and cold and only likes his stall for the night hours. He wanders around our yard during the day where I try to keep him from eating my flowers. He stands close by the big windows of our house to take his naps and likes to be wherever the sun is.

We only had three chickens as summer ended. One froze and the hawk ate one for breakfast this winter. Our remaining one has a little house on the end of our barn and all winter we keep a light shining on the roost to keep her warm. I only open her door if it is 20 degrees or warmer.

After they eat and drink, they hide under the big horse barn to be safe from eagles and hawks to be warm. And our 8-foot high garden fence has kept moose and bears out of their yard.

You were so kind to send NC gifts our way.

Marilyn Skau   **email June 4, 2016**

Ben Kaniut employee/ "receptionist"

The very first time I saw and met Pam, was when she walked into Ben's office. She reminded of the most beautiful little China doll I had ever seen.

As I got to know her, her naivety, innocence and most of all her goodness were so refreshing and such a pleasure to be around. She is one of the most generous people I have ever known. Being the recipient of many a gift from Pam—my Christmas horse, cards, letters, phone calls, invitations to her home and the monetary gifts— always came at a time when I needed each of them the most. She is such a God send.

She is also an exceptional cook. My favorite dish she made for me was rabbit. I have always enjoyed rabbit but her style of fixing it was exceptional.

It was a very lucky day for me when Pam came into my life and I will always be thankful for her friendship.

Jean Adams   **email July 4, 2016 Hi Larry**

Pam You are a Beautiful Woman;

As I write this my thoughts go back to when we first met in 2011. I have visited with you two times since then; you have become a dear, dear friend.

Pam, you were there when I said goodbye to my parents. You helped me cope when I needed a friend to talk to regarding serious

72

family and life issues. Hearing from you through letters and phone calls; telling me what was happening with you and yours made me feel I was part of your family.

When I was going through sad times I remember going to the Post Office. I was not expecting to receive a letter but I did; you cheered me on and strengthened my resolve to not give up. Your only request was for me to stay in contact; you were even patient with me when I was in school; and I wrote during breaks. You helped me learn what God said about unconditional love; a new way to live. I was not afraid you would judge my character even when I thought I could not tell anyone about my driving incident.

Some day I hope to see you again; I want you to know you are in my heart. I feel your presence even when we cannot be together in Alaska, a land we both love.

I love you.

Sue Francis

Pam, Thank you for your Christ-like example of what it means to follow Christ wholeheartedly. Your love, prayers and commitment to Christ, Larry, your family and friends has spoken volumes to me. I have watched you put a smile on your face and be a servant to others even when you were suffering physically yourself. You always see the good in others and have a heart/tongue that desires to honor the Lord and others. You love to be creative in so many ways and it is always fun to see the joy you bring to others. Your love for animals, nature, gardens, outdoors was another way God drew our hearts together. I have been encouraged as I have watched your continual selfless attitude along with your strong faith in the Lord, be your strength and hope even when life is difficult. Thank you for enriching my life by being my friend, sister in Christ and prayer support over the years!

Love you lots!
Sue Francis.

LARRY SAYS

The internal beauty that radiates from your soul surpasses even your eye-popping physical beauty; your beauty flows from the fount of God's beauty, touching and beautifying everything within your presence.

Crafts

Pam has always involved kids and ladies with her baking-cooking: Melinda, Heidi and Lynette Baer, Lonita. She had kids crack eggs, open-empty them, stir and touch.

Pam also had kids open jars, etc., put stuff in garbage, touch-feed-groom horse, chicks, ducks, geese; making bed. She enjoyed giving kids the opportunity they may have otherwise missed.

August 25, 2000

Last night as I held a sandwich sized zip-lock bag for Pam, she scraped baked ham into it. The ham consisted mostly of pieces or scraps. I assumed that she was going to save them for soup. I began thinking of the sweet, kind attitude and the thriftiness of this lady over the years.

She's never had the luxury of buying and tossing.

And she's never had the attitude of wasting things. She's very frugal and is the epitome of good stewardship.

When she prepares a turkey, she uses everything off the bird that could possibly be used...with the exception of the bones. We don't make our own girdles nor pierce our ears or noses, so we have no use of the bones. The turkey is eaten at a meal then refrigerated to be used until it is gone. Nearly always after a few days in the frig, Pam removes the meat and places it into zip-lock bags for sandwiches and/or soup, then freezes portions.

It is common for her to make a soup by boiling the flesh and fat from the bird and using everything that falls off the bones.

It is incredible being married to a lady who is so thoughtful. She does not bake a bird, eat once and toss into the garbage.

And she recycles many other things. We eat berries and turn "left overs" into jelly, jam or include in cooking.

September 5, 2002 She chose me—like the Mannequin movie—the Egyptian girl chose the window dresser. Pam chose me. How fortunate could I be?

Her unselfish love has never wavered. She put the Lord first. Then me. Then our children. The church people. The neighbors. Always doing something for someone. Writing 30 or more letters a month, longhand and without repetition.

Baking and cooking for others.

Making May baskets every year for neighbors—Hammans, Stuits, Baers, Millers—and friends—Rosemary.

Taking eggs to Steve Couture and Jean; Nancy and Tim behind us (9/02).

Always thinking of others who needed encouragement or support—Carl Snyder, Al Smay, Jody Garcia, Ralph Ertz, Tamara, Mike McKinley. Inviting them to our home for picnics or special times at Christmas or Thanksgiving.

Pam's cooking skills—many recipes, variety of food—plan to always have balanced meals, good/healthful food, 1970's—no sugar, 1999+ organic.

Relationship with God parallels Christ and church.

Health: Pam has been exposed to or affected by hypoglycemia, fibromyalgia, chronic fatigue Lyme's disease, multiple organ "failures" and dysautonomia. She has victoriously faced discouragement, disappointment and depression.

Pam's mother Hazel had their "lake" (a Columbia River slough near Park Rose/Portland) sprayed with DDT, two years in a row. It adversely affected Pam and her siblings.

When Pam was in college, she chose to lose weight but damaged her health in so doing.

In the early 1970's she had hypoglycemia and had to eat protein every couple of hours—peanut butter and/or cheese.

Pam has learned her body's language and through careful monitoring, knows she can stand for a half hour at a time. During what she refers to as "my down time," she writes letters or engages in other activities that allow her to regain her strength. It seems she does as much or more than healthy women, in spite of her health issues.

In the late 1970's we went to Virginia Mason Clinic in Seattle, a disappointing endeavor since the docs told her that her health was psychosomatic. In 1982 we went to the University of Alabama Hospital where she was diagnosed as having dysautonomia and prescribed drugs that nearly killed her before she stopped taking them. Later around 2014 she was so ill coughing that she asked me one night to "shoot me." I made an appointment with an alternative chiropractor I'd been seeing. I took her to him and he validated her health issues as having adrenals and thyroid that crashed, flat worms in her heart, parasites and over 300 allergies.

We worked with our youth at church in the 1970's—Wednesday nights, a canteen on Saturday evenings and Sunday mornings. How did she manage? She managed.

Pam always has time for everyone. When she's in the middle of something at home and the doorbell rings, guess what? She answers it, welcomes in the visitor and offers them something to drink or eat—coffee, tea, orange juice, cookies, muffins.

I remember around 1975 when she got breakfast for Ginger, Jill, Ben and me, prepared lunches, saw us off then lay on a mattress on the living floor with Ben until she recovered enough to tackle the rest of the day, which included lunch for Ben and her and dinner for the family.

Her family's health and welfare always remained number one for Pam.

Nicknames:

- Angle (Face)
- Birthday Girl
- Brunhilda
- Lover Girl
- Diane
- Pammy Pooh
- Snickerdoodle
- T.B/Tundra Bunny
- Tootsie Woodles
- Gertie
- Gretchen
- Hiledgard
- Maggie
- OG (Old Girl)
- Pooskkie Wooskie
- Specious
- Timmy
- Gertrude
- Helen
- J.B. / Jabber Box
- Pamela
- Pammy
- Rose
- Strawberry Nose
- Tootsie

Energizer Bunny pretty well describes her non-stop activities.

Pam is a faithful and righteous woman. Always tries to treat others as she thinks Jesus would.

She loves gardening...even pulling weeds. One day a neighbor girl was here while Pam plucked long grass from the front lawn and put it into her boots so that she could give it to Prince; but the little neighborhood girl removed it, thinking it was messing up Pam's boots. Pam loves kids, grandkids, flowers.

Writing old folks: Around 1993 or so Pam sat in her brother Craig's house, holding his mother-in-law's hand. Emma Wilson's husband Virgil had passed and Pam tried to comfort her. Pam thought it would be good to write Emma because she was alone. Before you know it, Pam was writing five octogenarians, including her Uncle Johnny. As time passed and these folks departed, she chose others...writing 2-5 page long-hand letters to each, every week. I finally talked her into letting me put them into the computer and print out copies. She now writes 20 to 30-plus on a regular basis... including Karen Kendall and her mother Lou Buchaltz, Jean Adams, Ronnie Kineen, Marilyn Skau, Don Mencl, Helen Timmons, Carol Espedal, Melinda Skieens, JoAnna Di Carlo and her mother Billie.

Pam identifies with all ages, from tiny tots to senior citizens. From the multitudes of church kids, former students of mine, neighbors and others, Pam loves them all. She's always finding someone else to adopt, like Bonie Hemry's grandchildren Joseph and Christine.

Pam's signature pansy on pie, muffin or cookie plates.

Pam likes to cover framed pictures with others she chooses.

She likes to seasonally decorate: fall is orange, pumpkins; Christmas is red-green with wreaths, snowmen; spring is white with flowers, swags and lots of flowers. She loves flowers inside or outside.

Her desire to show folks the yard, especially her horse and barn

Grandkids (Pam wrote)

1)   Sarah's Tiny House...movement on May 9, 2017

   12:10   on Kaniut's driveway

   12:15   by grandpa's study

12:30 unhooked from pickup

12:45 Bobcat hooking up to house

12:50 turned bobcat off

12:51 Bobcat hooking up and pulling house north

12:53 plywood onto ground

12:58 moving house lots of wood under house

12:59 House going north again, more wood underneath

1:01 swinging house to west; Bobcat left running; lady here talking to Brad

1:03 motor off

1:04 Bobcat on, moving house

1:11 finished moving to back

1:13 Bobcat going again, moved a bit, up and down—wiggle, wiggle; added more boards

1:20 Bobcat off

1:22 moving house again—to the north, house tipped up a little

1:25 Bobcat leaving

1:31 removing oversize sign on tiny house

Thank you, Lord and Brad for Sarah's precious tiny house.

Family

Vivian Lenore Kralman Jenkins   May 1996 poem

I haven't had the privilege of knowing Pam well.
What I know I will happily tell.
She's loving, compassionate, and kind as can be.
She's as near an angel that an earthling will see.
When Larry got married, I didn't lose a son,
I gained another daughter so I really won.
As near as I know, Pam has never been well;
She gave Larry three children and they turned out swell.
I wish health and bushels of happiness to come her way
To strengthen and brighten her every day.

Ginger (Kaniut) Risch   "4 book on mom" note (1996 ?)

Grandmamushky is the most recent endearment for my loving mother. There have been many others over my twenty-seven years.

"Strawberry Nose" has spent the last twenty-five years of her life constantly ill. Often she looks healthy as she looks much younger than her age, and people can't understand what an incredible last twenty-five years she has lived.

Many times she is so ill she is in bed for weeks, or perhaps she may only stand fifteen minutes and then rest 30-60 minutes. Yet she

79

has put her trust and salvation in God, choosing to be happy and playful instead of complaining, bitter and depressed.

This has always amazed me as most people complain plenty when sick with a cold or flu, however mom—even in severe pain and having trouble breathing and walking—would not complain.

Being as close to mom as I am, I know it hasn't been easy for her to be sick, physically or emotionally. Many doctors told her that her problems were mental. Never have I seen a more balanced person; however the doctors have not been able to heal her, thus they have said it's in her head.

Mom has always been one to be active—milking cows and riding horses for fun as a teen…seeing others hiking mountains and riding horses and not being able to must have been extremely frustrating for her.

Instead of dwelling on her limitations and feeling sorry for herself, mom has done for others on a daily basis. She baked cookies, bread or prepared a meal for others—neighbors and friends.

Mom's cooking has always been great and she prepared three nutritious meals a day for her family. Mom and dad set a good example for us having others over Sundays, evenings and holidays. Doing so even when it was difficult for mom; and finances were a creative challenge.

Housework was not overlooked and as myself and my sister and brother grew up, mom trained us to help with the dusting and dishes and vacuuming and such.

I remember weak that she was, mom would talk to others on the phone, calling to check on people and to listen (counsel as we would call it). Many, many letters have been sent to loved ones, friends and acquaintances as on her down time when she was strong enough, mom would write letter after letter. What a blessing for people to receive news from their old neighborhood and city while away at college and far from family.

Always being there for family and friends—to watch a horse show, read an English paper, to encourage or to lend a listening ear has meant so much to myself and so many people who know how kind and caring mom remains through each day, each year.

God blessed me with a Godly mother who continues to put others first no matter the cost and who taught me to know God.

Mom's love, listening, giving helping, gifts, jokes and patience have been main characteristics people see.

As Romans 8:28 says, "And we know that all things work together for good to them that love God, to them who are called according to His purpose." I know it is so with my mother—who has provided a sound example of Jesus and His teachings for those in and out of her life each day. Her life continues to be an inspiration.

Brad Risch

As for the Pam Book, "I have given it thought and while I could write a paragraph or a page or even a whole book I always came around to a singe word; LOVE. Pamela is Love."

Sarah Risch

I was so excited to go to M-bar-D. What horse crazy girl wouldn't be? Even if I didn't walk out of there with something new, the horse store was always an experience one loves to relive. None of us knew however, that there was going to be an extensive process to pick out a bridle for Prince, which in turn would change the course of both our lives. I walked into that store as a single child with only outdoor pets. Over the two hours of bridle shopping, I made friends with a furry four legged. You walked out of M-bar-D with a beautiful bridle. I walked out with a very special, free kitten.

Fast forward nine years and that cute cat got to live with you. Fast forward another two years, and again, that special kitty was able to reside in your home. I am forever thankful for your and grandpa's generosity and putting up with so much over the years. I had the best of times at your house, whether it was for the day or an overnight slumber party.

One thing I was always excited for were the lists. They were very balanced lists containing activities, chores to help out with and food choices for the day. We would always be outside if we could, but if the weather didn't allow the roller skates would be brought out, the table moved over and the kitchen (and other parts of the house) converted into a roller rink! Badminton, croquet and playing with Prince where always some outside favorites.

Once the tree house was built we used a trolley system with a bucket to get things from the kitchen up to the fort. In the winter we would hook Diogenes up to the dog sled and go for short rides. You taught me to talk to bugs, not be afraid of daddy longlegs and use cooking knives at the prime age of two-years-old. I was also taught the importance of not crying when my mom came to pick me up but instead be happy to see her and be thankful I had the time that I did at your house. There are many wonderful memories floating around in my head. Thank you for being a key person in my upbringing. You have taught me many life's lessons, both big and small. You have taught me the importance of love, generosity, perseverance and a positive attitude. Thank you for everything!! Love you much, "Fluffy"

Jill Kaniut February 5, 2018

Pamela Diane

A mother.

A woman of virtue.

A friend, a neighbor, an aunt and a wife.

She never raised her temper, swore, smoked, drank or spoke harshly.

She is a quiet woman with gratitude. She would play the piano occasionally, always hymns which sat propped up, held open with clothespins.

She would keep a clothespin on her sweater and often a Kleenex up her sleeve cuff.

She taught us what it meant to sacrifice. She did it without words. She would wear our hand-me-downs and rarely spend money on herself. She never went to the "beauty parlor;" she never had her hair done or a manicure.

Sometime in the 1990's I started calling her Helen. She never seemed to mind.

She loved old westerns: Dale Evans, Roy Rogers and anything that had to do with horses, cowboys or westerns. She loved her horses Duke and Prince. She loved to hold the cat Julie on her lap out in the yard in the winter.

She was always quick to accept and like everyone. There was never a neighbor, former student, repairman, ferrier or postman who came into our home my mom didn't say, "Oh, he is the nicest man."

She didn't always speak of hope, but she lived hope. Teaching us to believe God was very good.

She lived the verse "do not complain or grumble." Led a quiet life at home. Did not gossip.

She is the most sweet person I know. Animals and people alike loved her.

If you came to visit in the summer, you could depend upon a tour of the yard with stops at the garden and a basket of fresh eggs to go home with or maybe an armful of rhubarb or a handpicked cluster of flowers or mint.

She had a way about her that put everyone at ease in her company and when you were in her presence you felt validated and important.

She loved to write letters to people and communicate that they mattered. She made them feel loved and remembered. No one seemed to care about the misspelled words or the tedious updates about the horse or yard happenings. Her letters rarely required an answer but transported her friends briefly back to her quiet farm world.

She loved to send plates of baked goods to the neighbors. She felt badly if she did not welcome a new neighbor punctually.

Neighborhood children saw her more like Mary Poppins than

Mrs. Claus. She would always prioritize visitors with something to eat or drink.

She would drag out glue and markers, paper and stickers for the child to do a "craft."

In the 1970's and 80's it was customary for 3-5 loaves of freshly baked bread to be resting on the tile counter when school was out. All the children in the neighborhood over the years knew that meant a thick slice of bread with melting butter.

During the years of my childhood I didn't realize how poor we were. Her generously sharing hard pasta noodles so we could glue it on paper must have been hard knowing that could be "dinner."

She didn't make us feel poor, and we didn't really know we were. She validated and valued us and put us to bed at night by feeding our imaginations with "make up stories" she would create to give us such happiness.

She is a loyal, faithful, thoughtful friend.

She likes to keep lists and share information with us. You could expect a "list" of things she would keep, intending to go over them with you when you stopped by the house.

She loved phone calls from Oregon. Especially from her brothers.

She loved almond Rocca, lemon drops and anything that looked like chocolate or tasted like it.

She told us raison cookies were good for breakfast and she could often be found eating chocolate chips at all times during the day.

She kept pictures of every friend and taped them up on her wall, updating it each time she got a new one.

The day started with cleaning the bathroom…every day.

She never missed an opportunity to tell everyone they needed to be in church.

There may never have been a woman so sweet in all the world.

I am very blessed to have had the incredible woman, mother and dear friend. She blessed me in too many ways to count. She is difficult to describe because her tender spirit is more than amazing. She well represents the comparison of Christ. The love of a Father, caring more for us than words can express.

      I love you, Moms!

        --Jill

(more input from **Larry**)...Pam always involves kids, trying to make them feel comfortable. For instance, if we were having curly fries, she picked different grandchildren to peel potatoes, prepare them, turn the crank on the cutting machine.

Ben Kaniut and family Mother's Day card May 8, 2016 (You make the world a more lovely place to be)

Momma, Thank you for all of the love you have poured into my life, through my life. And, thank you for all of the love you give to my wife and boys. You truly make the world a lovelier place. **Ben**

Pam, Thank you for your kindness, generosity and warm spirit. Thank you for loving on the boys and spending time with them, teaching them and encouraging them. Happy Mother's Day. Much love, Heather P.S. Thanks for being a wonderful mother to my husband and your son. **Heather**

Have a great Mother's day! Love you! **Logan**

Grandma Pam, Hope you have fun on mother's day. Today a day of May. Hip hip Horrah for Mother's Day! **Preston Kaniut**

Grandma Pam, Thank you for letting us come over. Hope we can come sometime soon. Happy Mother's Day. Love, **Cannon**

Lincoln loves you, you are the best Grandma in the world. **Lincoln**

    REUBEN

Laura Lee Smothers March 2005 e-mails

The first time Les and I saw Pam was in 1960 when Kelly was three months old. January found us with Kaniut and Pam on our way to Mt. Hood for the Warner Pacific Snow day. I had Kelly wrapped warmly, because we didn't have any Alaska clothes in those days. If I remember right Kaniut had his book and clipboard with him and Pam was dressed in a beautiful white jacket. We invited them over to our little tiny place after we returned. We had a nice time, but when they left, I told Les, "We'll never see her again." We were pretty sure that she would be looking for someone like Robert Redford or Roy Rogers. Had I known what her dad was like I would have realized that Kaniut and Howard were a lot alike in some ways. Determined.

(One time when I was going through a tough time, Howard sent me a wonderful note telling me how much he appreciated me and was proud of me. I had never received such a letter from my own dad, so it was really meaningful.)

The next major event I remember was when Les, Dad Smothers, an African student and I went to San Francisco for a minister's meeting. There is no way we could have done that if Pam hadn't taken care of Kelly. I think Kelly was 18 months old. That is probably when Kelly fell in love with Pam. She has always respected her and thought of her as a mom mode. I think we were gone about 5 days total and Pam survived. That was the first time we left Kelly like that. We took our kids with us most everywhere we went. Pam was living at home then so Kelly probably had a ball watching them feed the hogs and sheep and do the other things that make a farm memory lasting.

It seems like Pam had already started having problems with her health when she was at college before they got married. I appreciate the tips she picked up when she worked for some time for a florist during college years or when they were first married. She has given many ideas through the years and I have admired the many special arrangements and bouquets that she has given to innumerable others. She was always including her children in projects and how to do things, so it is natural for them to be such sharing and creative kids.

I remember Pam telling about walking with the children with a sled or wagon. I think it was a sled, and she decided to lay across the kids when she felt that a local moose might be threatening them.

On August the 28th I bounced Pam and Ben over the bumpy roads to the hospital. I was living on the property with our camper and Pam came out and told me she thought it wouldn't be long before she needed to go to the hospital. I think she waited quite a while in view of the fact that this was her third delivery and they usually come a lot more rapidly than the earlier ones. We had a gaudy Dodge four wheel drive truck that was three quarter ton, so it had heavy springs. A Cadillac it was not. We called Kaniut at Dimond High to let him know we were on the way to the hospital so he could meet us there. I imagine that will be the first and last time I hold someone's hand and steer with the other while we are rushing her to delivery. Pam was there very briefly before they took her into delivery. They gave the father a gown and left the chauffeur sitting outside wondering how things were going. It was a good place to pray for the mom, baby, dad and attendants. What a fantastic present for their anniversary. A new baby and the first boy!

You can imagine what it was like coming up the Alcan that 1973 summer with Pam being very expectant. Les and I and Kelly slept in the camper on the bed above the cab. Pam, Larry, Ginger and Jill slept on the bed made with the table and built in benches. I don't know how they slept in that small space but I didn't hear any whining from Pam. Kent slept on the floor in a sleeping bag. He celebrated his fifth birthday on that trip. Pam and Larry had must bought a new Ford pickup and we had our 3/4 Dodge. Kaniut had our earthly possessions loaded in the back of his truck and we had plenty crammed into our camper. We were all on an adventure.

It rained all the way to Anchorage. We talked about selling maps to potholes, knowing they would change before another car passed through.

We were very thankful to have a kind sister-in-law when we perched on their property off and on from June until January of 73 to 74. We lived in our camper with a tent at the back of it for storage, but I'm sure we spent plenty of time pestering Pam. Kent and Ginger and Jill were close in age, so I know it must have been heaven for him to be able to play with his cousins since Kelly was 8 years older and into "mature" life by then.

Kaniut told us there was a job—several job openings in his high school so we stepped out on faith and moved up there. Les taught in the same school with Kaniut for eight years, Dimond High.

I didn't realize that Pam was a horsewoman and had experience on the farm. When I see anything with Roy Rogers and Dale Evans, I think of Pam and her horse.

I prayed twenty-five years for Pam's healing and asked the Lord how t o pray one day when the Lord said, "My responsibility is to do the healing and yours is to continue praying." So I continue praying for healing and wisdom. It is truly amazing that Pam doesn't get depressed. Somehow she must have reconciled herself to living a moment at a time and being thankful for the amount of strength she does have. It is amazing to me how much she was able to be a counselor to neighbors and others who knew she had a listening ear. (I still owe her for my counseling bills!) Had she not had the medical problems, she would not have had time to work with so many people along the way because she might have been working outside the home to help with the finances.

She worked at making a dollar stretch. I enjoyed going berry picking with Pam and Kaniut. They never left the kids or had babysitters, so that was a great way to save money. Kaniut worked summers commercial fishing and construction to keep the wolf away from the door. Pam and the kids and Larry did a lot of hand made gifts and cards continually. Not just for Christmas. We received many special gifts. One that I love is a bunch of grapes that Pam made for her mom of burgundy colored velour or velvet. When Hazel passed away, Pam sent those grapes to me. I really loved them and it was wonderful to have something that belonged to Hazel.

A couple of years into our Anchorage days, Les got a small moose and a sheep on separate hunting treks with Kaniut. Since we were house sitting at that time, we cut and packaged the animals at Kaniut's. Pam is usually in the midst of packaging things and I marvel at her willingness to be up at all hours finishing the many projects like that which come from varying friends.

When Hazel passed away, I went to their estate to see if I could help Pam. The family had chosen the things they wanted and Pam asked me if I would like to take anything that was left. I asked her if she minded my just walking around one last time. Our family had many wonderful experiences there through the years and it was really hard to realize that this was the end of our spending time with the elder Timmons or probably any of the local Timmons. It was the end of an era. Pam was very kind to understand how I was feeling. It was nice to be able to help even a little bit in the work of getting things cleaned up. Pam was able to help Ali and I feel a part of the family even though she was busy trying to superintend and do the work of dealing with the left overs.

Pam reached out to Kent in some fun ways. Because of my efforts to avoid sugar and yeast, my family didn't get a lot of sweets and carbos from me. Pam took pity on Kent and gave him a birthday present when he was about 8 that included homemade bread and a cube of butter monthly—which the rest of the family salivated over every month.

Pam and Larry took in Les' nephew for some time. He came up to spend some time with Mom and Dad Smothers and was there during the time we were building a home up on the mountain looking out at Mt. McKinley (1976). Pam tried to mentor him and mother him and help him to be part of their family…to have structure in his life. He was past school age or not attending and an older teen. She had a hard time getting him to bed at a decent hour, away from the television, getting him up in the mornings and trying to give him direction.

Since Kaniut was teaching school, the daytime efforts fell to Pam and what the kids might be able to do to encourage him. He enjoyed baking bread with Pam and just being there. I'm sure it was the first time he ever had a happy family life. He went back home after that.

Pam and Larry took in another young man who was basically ostracized by his parents. He was a student of Kaniut's. Had either Pam or Larry been unwilling to reach out to people and be hospitable as they were, the Kaniut family rancho would not have been able to enrich their "world" as they did. Les and I have felt for a long time that Pam and Larry should start a bed and breakfast because they are providing one anyway. No one can come to their home without eating something—regardless of how brief their stay.

Pam was always thinking of spontaneous as well as planned ways to bless people in a concrete way. She and Kaniut were very accepting of a neighbor with mental difficulties and made sure he and his family were invited to special gatherings like the Fourth of July and Thanksgiving. They consistently sent him food and notes and included him in social situations as much as possible. Pam was always very comfortable in instructing people around her if she thought she could help them improve, so he got a few lessons in civility and socialization and just basic normal ways to behave. I know it helped his children to be included in a family situation. I tried having him to our home, but Les had difficulty with strong comments and ideas, making Les uneasy to have him around, so we pretty much stuck to the times we were invited to the Kaniut's when the neighbor was there. They still keep in touch with this man and probably have been more faithful even than his family in supporting him and his boys through the years.

During the summer after we started "camping out" in Anchorage we left at four one morning with a very pregnant Pam for another adventure. We had all our kids and Kaniut's two in the little hatchback Kaniuts owned. We traveled over the pass to Ninilchik and went clamming with Oregon to Alaska friends of theirs, the Lindemans. Larry earned his masters while interning at Renne Junior High in Newberg, Oregon. John coached wrestling and mentored Larry and Delores was the school secretary. Lindemans had a large family and a fairly self-contained farm. Though John taught school and coached, they more or less lived off the land. Pam was pretty close to delivering Ben so Delores and Kelly took Kent and me for a horseback ride. It was fun fellowshipping with friends of Pam and Larry and feeling a part of another Alaskan homestead family.

The winter of 1973 to 1974 we followed the Kaniuts in their Volkswagen, we in our mustard yellow Dodge, through every back alley short cut in Anchorage to the Fur Rendezvous Parade. February in Alaska is something like Mardi Gras in New Orleans. It's the major parade of the year in Alaska, complete with horn players with their lips stuck to their instruments! (Rondy now includes the running of the reindeer as well as the outhouse race and snowshoe softball). We had homemade chili and hot chocolate and sandwiches..

Although Pam was nursing Ben, she and I decided to leave him in the truck with Kaniut and Les while she and I stood on the parade route for a closer "look see." We wore warm parkas and Alaska duds so we were having a hilarious time watching the "spectacular" in spite of rosy cheeks. We were aware of the keystone cops and their portable jail which was periodically filled with people who had not purchased Fur Rendezvous buttons. We laughed about how funny it would be if they arrested us because we couldn't afford the buttons for our little herd. About that time they arrested us. I didn't think it appropriate to put a nursing mom in jail but we weren't in the calaboose long and Ben was delighted to have his mother return for his next feeding.

It was really a wonderful experience.

We ventured on many berry picking outings and learned they evolved into delicious jelly at the hands of Pam's expertise. Pam and Larry also taught us about fiddle head ferns. They are great dipped in a light batter and deep fried. Since the early 1970's Pam became more aware of healthy food and adjusted her menus accordingly.

Les and Izzy Polzin   March 26, 2005 letter

Pam to us is a true sister in the Lord—she believes in prayer and has several times asked us to pray for someone or a need close to her heart. We value her friendship.

Besides she is also the mother of our favorite granddaughter by marriage to our number one grandson (first born). That alone would endear her to our hearts.

Kim Speegle   April 18, 2016

It's too bad my mom's not around. She would have loved to

contribute to it. I know that my mom always enjoyed all the letters and phone calls from Pam over the years. It meant so very much to her.

Good luck with the book.

Linda Monsarrat   thank you card c. March/April 2016

Dear Pam,

For the first time I went to the Post Office alone yesterday and found such a special treat in my box—your lovely card and letter of love and encouragement. Thank you so much for all you have done for me these past six months—the lovely white flower arrangement, the cards, treats—all so yummy, the picture of Homer, and most of all the prayers. (Pam wanted Linda to have a note the first time she went to the post office in her new home.)

Carole Espedal   April 25 (mailed), 2016 letter

Larry, How fortunate you are to have such a kind, caring, loving wife. Pam's Uncle Clarence thought she was the sweetest of his nieces. I agreed with him. At Christmas she always takes time to let me know what has been going on with your family. All the time I have known her she has been in poor health but doesn't let that stop her. I have never heard her complain. I am glad you are taking the time to let the world known how lucky you are.

Sincerely,
Carole Espedal

Emma and Virgil Wilson   February 19, 1996 letter

Dear Larry,

In respond to your letter, Virgil and I doing fine wishing it wasn't so far up there, stop say hello! Wishing Pam was close by, her cheery smile, she love to walk out round in yard looking and smelling all flowers enjoying outdoors so much. Walk down the road talking about every little details on the trees and scrubs. She loves to do craft. She always love see what you're serving or making, another special things is cooking. She love to share what she have in recipes.

When you give a gift you don't have to go over board giving, she happy what you have to give she appreciated and enjoy it. I seen a little piece in paper, "Of all the friends I could ever make you're truly the icing on the cake."

Bill & Jean Ellsworth   April 14, 2005 letter

From the first time I met Pam at Grandma Hazel's, to phone conversations and letters, she (Pam) has been an inspiration with her quiet, gentle, calm, caring kind, logical ways and attitude.
I've enjoyed all her letters about family, horses, gardens, Alaska, and, all the pictures to go with it.

Also having read most of all the bear books Larry has written helps see the in between of their Alaskan life.

I would say Pam is a blessing—with a wonderful family and having some wonderful siblings also.

God bless you all,
Jean Ellsworth

Larry Kaniut's letter   February 15, 1992   from a letter

Pam still the sweetest thing I know. Told me yesterday as we delivered Valentine's gifts that she'd made, "When I'm able to make someone feel good, I don't feel so worthless." That was on the way home from renewing her driver's license and handicapped sticker. I told her it was kind of ironic that we were renewing since she never drives…to which she replied, "I've lost so much body strength and ability to do things that it gives me a false sense of security to think I can drive. It gives me hope that I haven't lost everything."

Just after that she told me that she is noticing she's having more trouble with her short term memory. She's a concerned, if not frightened, lady. She's tried so hard to get well so she can do more for those she loves. She also told me that she's thinking very seriously about getting off all medication and shots because she has noticed no improvement… "I've felt pretty terrible since Christmas, and the medical treatment seems like a waste of money." I keep remembering how I teased her dad, "If Pam doesn't get better, I'm going to have to sue you for child support."

The above comments of Pam's are a silent cry of frustration and discouragement. Need to focus more attention, effort and prayer on her. I love that girl with the hazel eyes and auburn hair.

First lady honors 20 Alaska volunteers

The Associated Press

JUNEAU — First lady Michael Cowper has honored 20 volunteers for their service in communities statewide.

The winners were selected from 116 volunteers nominated for the annual First Lady's Volunteer Awards presented last month.

A five-member citizens' panel selected the winners.

A special award also will be given to Kay Linton of Anchorage, who has helped coordinate the volunteer awards program during most of the past 10 years.

This year's 20 winners are:

• Skeeter Jepson of Kotzebue, active in emergency medical services and search-and-rescue activities;

• Carrol Martin of Soldotna, a 4-H club leader for 16 years and a member of the Kenai Peninsula State Fair Board;

• Dr. Doug Weaver of Juneau, a Big Brother for the past 10 years and member of the Tongass Community Counseling Center;

• Alicia Iden of Anchorage, board president of the Anchorage Center for Families and a member of the Alaska Mental Health Board;

• Kathy Amon of Seward, whose activities include Girl Scouts, Boy Scouts and hospital work;

• Jane MacKinnon of Juneau, a seven-year hospice volunteer and a Hospital Guild member for 15 years;

• Linda Johnson of Anchorage, a seven-year veteran of a 24-hour crisis line for sexual-assault victims;

• Meg Gaydosik of Fairbanks, an 11-year member of an agency to assist domestic-violence victims;

• Jim Pate of Anchorage, 15 years old, who suffers from asthma and has helped other children cope with the disorder;

• Dr. Dennis Swarner of Kenai, a 12-year Lions Club member who also is active in 4-H;

• Sadie Brower Neakok of Barrow, who volunteers as an English-Inupiat translator;

• Pamela Diane Kaniut of Anchorage, who provides counseling services and free homemade gifts for people;

• Joy Griffin of Homer, active in community library programs;

• Tess Young of Anchorage, who donates more than 1,000 hours a year to greeting visitors;

• Celeste Benson of Anchorage, a 12-year member of the Fairview Community Council;

• Fred Walstka of Anchorage, Southcentral director for the March of Dimes Alaska chapter;

• James Crockett of Anchorage, treasurer for Bean's Cafe, a homeless shelter;

• Loreen Steeves of Upper Kalskag, who promotes cultural heritage through a 4-H program;

• Vivian Dietz-Clark of Anchorage, who has volunteered as a tutor, foster parent, choir chaperon and costume maker; and,

• Jackie Fett of Delta Junction, who helps with computer work, health tests, spelling bees and band classes at schools.

JUNEAU — First lady Michael Cowper has honored 20 volunteers for their service in communities statewide.

The winners were selected from 116 volunteers nominated for the annual First Lady's Volunteer Awards presented last month.

A five-member citizens' panel selected the winners.

A special award also will be given to Kay Linton of Anchorage, who has helped coordinate the volunteer awards program during most of the past 10 years.

This year's 20 winners are:

• Pamela Diane Kaniut of Anchorage, who provides counseling services and free homemade gifts for people;

Activities

A glimpse of Pam's daily activities includes: getting up, cleaning bathroom and house, arranging household furniture; preparing three scrumptious meals from scratch; providing goodies for others; prayer list essential each day; washing clothes by color—blue, white, red; cleaning kitchen before bedtime.

Summer: work flowers, dirt, weed yard, weed, picnic (incomplete without egg toss, 3-legged race), many who played—our kids, Joanna, Tamara, John, Barry, Brad, church and FCA kids from 1960's to 1980's. Winter: flower arrangements; prepare craft for kids—be they ours, our grandkids or visitors (create fun activity for them); ducks, geese, horses, dog, pig, garden, yard, barn, house; neighbors; attended-supported kids events, my coaching; frustration/concern re: her health which was day to day, often minute by minute; denture hassle and phlegm problem (embarrassment), allergies.

Pam has a history of telling our children "make ups" at bed time, making up a story that ended that night. She is also known for her creativity in the arena of crafts and always has some for the children, whether they be neighbors, family or visiting kids. One of her favorite activities with children is letting them configure a fort in the living room, using pillows from the couch and so forth.

January 21, 2001, Pam surprised us on her birthday. Pam told us that she had a present for us (after she opened all hers), proceeded to the piano and played a hymn that she has been practicing since

October when she decided that she wanted to learn to play the piano with both hands. She was "nervous" she said because "I knew I was performing." She hopes her efforts are an inspiration to Sarah to play.

Pam has always been a bundle of activity, from preparing and delivering May day flowers to neighbors—with our children, our grandchildren and neighbor kids—to Christmas caroling in and out of the neighborhood, visiting the sick, baking-delivering goodies and finding ways to encourage others. She's even been known to sing to her ducks, geese, rabbits, horse or pig, to visit the horse in his stall and to bring him grass she's plucked from the lawn.

When our girls had horses, Pam and the girls walked or drove a couple of blocks up 142nd and cropped wild grass from the neighbor-free area and brought it home for the girls' horses.

Pam Fights Back   October 2005

About a week before Valentine's Day Pam had a mini-adventure. She was walking down the hall by our bedroom when she spotted a cute, 4-legged shrew migrating from our old study to Ben's bedroom-new study. Needless to say she was not happy. She watched the critter slither over and around piles of paper and other objects mis-laid on the floor and she came up with a plan.

She figured it was just a matter of time before the cute little fuzz ball returned to her locale so she took off a boot with the intent of rendering the innocent little creature defuncto.

Before long, as Pam squatted with boot held hammer-like in right hand in a javelin thrower's position and watched, here comes the fuzz ball.

Whap!

Flat fuzz ball. No quiver. No nothing. Just a defuncto shrew.

She came to the kitchen to fetch her ever faithful husband, crooked her right index finger in a "follow me" motion and took me to see her trophy. Quite like the happy cat who's returning to the house with mouse in mouth.

Pam and her Sunday visitor   December 2005

Unsalted peanuts in the shell cluttered themselves about a fifteen-inch circle on our green metal table on the back deck. As Pam stood with back warming to the kitchen fireplace and looking out the bay window, a beautiful dark Steller's jay with black head lifted off the table flying toward the horseshoe pit, nut in beak. I'm wondering if it is Stanley from the summer of 2003 coming to renew his friendship. He hid the nut and returned to the table for more booty.

Then he launched east over our neighbor Steve Couture's cedar fence. In a short time he harkened back to the "come and get it" venue.

He coasted in, landed on the flower pot in the center of the table then hopped onto the table for another morsel. His next designation was the lawn adjacent to the iris patch and rose bush. There he rearranged a few dead leaves and deposited his peanut.

From the bay window Pam witnessed his next mission to the flower box outside the freezer window for another deposit.

Then she opened the back door and began putting on her boots and coat preparatory to going outside to feed the animals—Prince the horse, Diogenes the mixed breed canine and Banana, the Holstein painted cat, the latter two "adopted" to us by our son Ben. While looking out the opened door Pam watched Stanley fly to the tree fort, its floor twelve feet off the ground and fifteen feet behind the deck

Pam walked out and sat at one of the four green metal table chairs. In moments he flew in, landed on the flower pot again and hopped onto the table for a nut before flying off toward the power line bordering the back lawn.

Pam moved her chair closer to the table and wondered how long it would before Stanley returned. Just about then she felt something on her head and jumped, not knowing what it was. It was Stanley who had flown in from the front west side of our house.

She must have startled him as he flew away without a nut. Since he didn't return right away, Pam decided to do her chores. While at her work Pam saw him return, grab another peanut and head for the loft opening of the barn. He landed on the floor just above the ladder and disappeared for a couple of minutes.

In the meantime Pam went about her duties as chief animal husbandman, feeding and watering the animals, including the currently non-laying chickens.

When she returned to the table, all the peanuts were gone. And so was Stanley.

A Moo in the Night   2009

Pam asked me if I'd heard the sound of a tugboat moaning on the river.

"No. What did it sound like?"

"A low moaning. I've heard it a few times."

"When?"

"Today."

"What do you mean?"

"I've heard it a few times at different places in the house—by the water heater and in the kitchen and the bedroom."

We retired to the family room to watch a video. That's when I heard the lamentably sad moaning, *mooowwwaaaahhhhhh.* Momentarily stunned, our eyes riveted on each other.

I suggested maybe it was a moose outside the window. Or since I had worked on the incoming phone line earlier, maybe it was coming from that line.

Mooowwwaaahhhh.

Thinking it might be coming from the radio between us, I unplugged it and held it to my ear. No moan. Then I gave it to Pam.

Picture this: two geezers alternately holding a "dead" radio to their ears. No moaning.

I replaced the radio on the stand.

Mooowwwaaaahhhh. Not from the radio.

All of a sudden I detected the culprit. "Oh, it's Jill's cell phone on the stand by the radio."

So our daughter's cell phone tricked us both.

Are we Surrounded?   2010

What's that? Is someone having a problem? "Don't move. We've got you covered."

Maybe I was dreaming. No, there is someone talking. I climb out of bed. It's 5:15 A.M. Looked in old living room for radio noise. Not there. Looked out front window to see if someone is in the street. No one. Back to bedroom.

"Help. We need help."

Pam asked me if something were wrong. "No, I keep hearing noise and can't track it down. Maybe it's George getting ready to work and his barn radio is on."

Pam listened then suggested, "I think it's coming from one of the kid's toys. It's just outside our window. Remember those battery operated toys the grandsons left, the ones we stored under the eave? It must be one of those."

Sure enough. It was. How could those batteries be good outside in the cold this late in the winter? Hope they run down soon!

At 10 A.M. the next morning I went out and fetched the "Fix It" toy. It will either be delivered to Ben and Heather's so they can listen to it at 5 A.M. or it's going on a one way trip so the landfill operators can listen to it!

Mouse Caper   2011

Having spotted the quarry, the hunter raised his rifle and drew a fine bead on the animal. He hoped he could make a one shot kill and keep things as tidy as possible. It had been several years since he'd had a similar situation. He drew a deep breath and released it slowly as he pressured the trigger. *Pop*! The quarry vanished. Was it a hit? Or a miss? He comforted himself knowing that the target had been no more than six feet from the end of his barrel. He must have hit it!

Did I mention that he was shooting in his bathroom? A pellet gun? At a mouse?

Well, anyway, he discovered upon further viewing that he had cleanly missed the quarry...which hid behind the toilet next to a

Victor mouse trap which was baited with bird seed—glue gunned onto the trigger by the shooter's wife Pam.

Let's see. He spread a pair of socks beneath the door so the mouse couldn't get away. Since he couldn't see the critter, he moved a gallon vinegar bottle with the barrel of the rifle and saw the rodent. Another carefully aimed miss and the mouse was out of sight again. He wondered what to do. He was pretty sure that he'd hit it as he saw red and assumed it was blood. On further review he realized it was the red of the Victor trap and not blood. He didn't want to approach the little fuzz ball and scare it into escaping beneath the door. Was it still in the bathroom or had it found an escape route?

Next thing he knew he heard his wife outside the door asking what the rifle was doing leaning against the hall wall. He explained the situation and asked if she'd like to assist. He thought he could guard the door with his rolled up T-shirt while she moved toward the quarry—that if it got past her in its effort to escape, he could thump it with the shirt. She wasn't having any of it.

Minutes ticked away with no further mouse sighting. Finally Pam said she'd help and she started into the bathroom but suddenly asked if the mouse had run past her through the door opening.

The master of the house noticed that the little fur ball was hiding in a corner by the shower and had quickly skittered to the corner between the vanity and the toilet.

Pam started moving stuff from the shelf on the end of the vanity when the mouse barreled into high gear right past her legs and toward the master of the house who thumped, saw the mouse reverse course, thumped again and again as the critter scratched for a foothold when there was a *Whap!* from the sandal in Pam's hand.

The mouse quivered. "He's dead!" the master confirmed as he saw another striking sandal. "He's dead." *Whap!* "He's dead!" *Whap!*

She stopped abusing the little fellow and I congratulated her for her good aim.

Did I mention that it was 5 AM, early Halloween morning when we enjoyed our little mouse caper?

Radio Sportscaster...Prize fight announcer around 2011.

One night while babysitting Logan, Preston and Cannon at their Kempton Hills home, Pam announced the big fight of the evening... announcing the Austin Wolverine fighting the Old Man from Alaska. Logan had his boxing gloves and shared them with Preston. Each boy fought the Old Man from Alaska a few rounds, exchanging gloves. Between rounds Pam used a towel to fan the boxer who challenged the old guy. During each round she gave play by play as to how badly the kid was thrashing the geezer: "Hit him harder." "That's a good blow to the jaw." "Keep 'em coming." "You're wearing him out." Somewhere around the 8th round while the boys were trading gloves, the geezer felt a small fist landing on his jaw from the left. Cannon who was around 3-years-old sucker punched the geezer with a pretty good right to the jaw. We had a blast. The geezer was sitting with his back against the wall covering up with his arms protecting his face and trying not to laugh too hard. The boys punched away, having a good time beating up the geezer.

Zorilla rescue about 2016

On the way to church one cold, winter morning about 2016 we encountered a vehicle that we discovered was rented. There were 4 or 5 people and Pam thought we should invite them home until they could get their vehicle running. We left a couple there and took the husband and wife and one daughter to our home. They were visiting from California and immediately fell in love with the wonderful, thoughtful and generous Pam. She fixed them hot drinks and lunch and we visited until arrangements were made for the others to join us when their vehicle was on the road again.

We received a 2020 Christmas letter from the Zorilla's which stated in part: "Pam & Larry, Joe and I thank you for your letter. It was a pleasure to hear from you. We will never forget the time we spent in Alaska. My daughter said it was the best experience of her life."

Pam's note to Joanna Di Carlo (from July 2015)

So, here is what you've missed:

1. Lots of robins feeding worms to their twins on our lawn and in the garden, giving them 3-4 worms at a time

2. Lots of weeding — need you.

3. A weed patch turned into a pretty garden that turned into another weed patch.

4. Larry cleaning our plane Sunday on a lovely sunny afternoon while I read and wrote in the old Suburban, nearby. This week a man is going to look to buy—will see.

5. A plane landing on the mudflats by Birchwood.

6. A plane landing on Seward Highway by Potter's Marsh.

7. A 6 hour wait for travelers the night before the 4th on Seward Highway, Trooper ran over a motorcyclist who tried to evade him, struck a Suburban and was thrown into cop's path.

8. July 3rd a perfect day in a canoe with Jill, Jewel Lake. Relaxing—a no. 1 time

9. How excited I was last day of June when I finished editing the Roman soldier novel of Larry's.

10. An earthquake.

11. Two neighbor girls weeding--$1.00 an hour to raise money. They both want a horse.

12. Helping Larry, Ben and 5 grandboys hold down a tent in a 50 mph wind after biking 6 miles uphill. Wow! What fun? (Larry hadn't ridden a bike in a few years—did great)

13. Helping Ginger and I pack dishes, etc.

14. Ben's family and us at O'Malley Elementary playground for a picnic that Jill planned end of June.

15. Going to therapies with Ginger and Sarah.

16. Another special church service with Jill, Larry and me in Indian.

17. Watching the grandboys planting seeds in our garden—each had his own row.

Pam Says

Never seeing darkness day after day (from midnight to Easter)

A blessed and very special Easter memory is when Father created three crosses then took them to a high hill on our farm overlooking the Willamette Valley. Then he invited people from Dayton to come for a sunrise service.

Many years later my brother created a lighted cross, 40 feet tall, that stands permanently very near where those first crosses were.

CARDS

ANNIVERSARY

1) 47th Wedding August 25, 2011

She asked if I could think of a few words off the top of my head depicting her. I laughed because I couldn't limit myself to a few—there were dozens of words, too many to truly capture this auburn-haired, hazel-eyed beauty who took my hand in 1964, 47 years ago. I'm listing 47 descriptive words about her:

Attractive—one of the key remembrances of seeing her walk before WPC library. Long auburn hair, below her waist.

Well groomed

Cute

God-oriented—to be Godly has been her goal for years

Servant

Loyal—won't even tell me secrets others tell her

Faithful

Thorough—faithfully follows ingredients, plans to benefit others

Compassionate—cares deeply for others

Correspondent—writes faithfully over 30 letters (long hand) each month; great letter writer

Gentle—always putting others and their wishes before hers

Sweet—the adjective most used by others to describe her

Gourmet chef—no one can cook better

Utilitarian—makes do/makes use of everything; grandsons told their mother, "Don't throw away that fuzz, grandma can use it to make a craft."

Creative—makes up stories, games, fun crafts…she always has

Natural beauty—as always, my dream girl

Not cosmetic parlor—no need for makeup

Petite

Well dressed

Not clothes horse

Thrifty and Frugal—utilizes everything to the last gram

Easy to please

Thoughtful

Considerate

Kind

Friendly and neighborly

Good listener

Awesome grandmother

Comforter

Appealing

Good singer

Courageous

Brave

Generous

Giving-sharing

Wholesome

Romantic

Outstanding baker

Scintillating

Flair for perfection—flower arranger, petals on pie plate, egg yolk paintings, just the right touch

Animal lover

Talks and waves to the animals

Floral designer extraordinaire
Detail person

Loves yard work

Delicate, fragile, dainty

Happy Anniversary, Little Angel.

It has been my privilege to know you for 51 years…and to live with you for 47.

I Love You

BIRTHDAY

1) 70ᵀᴴ

Pamela Rose

It was many and many a year ago
     at a school house on a mount
     when a lady there went whom you all know
     by the name of Pamela Rose.

Her purpose for going to college then
     was strictly for snagging a mate.

She was eighteen and so was the guy
     who spotted her walking a friend.

Crystal Mock, her childhood pal, was no match for
     that sweet, kind Pamela Rose.
     With a gleam in his eye and a lump in his throat
     the guy watched the babes walk past.

Four months flew by when the guy took the gal
　　　　off to Timberline Lodge—
　　　　Mt. Hood beckoned and so did the car
　　　　　　to the beautiful Pamela Rose.

With a gleam in his eye and a lump in his throat
　　　　the guy cemented a goal.

In the year of our Lord, nineteen-sixty-four
　　　　the two young hearts became one—
pledging their love "till death do us part,"

　　　　　　Larry, the guy, chose Pamela Rose.
　　　　　　Then off to the North, Alaska's Great Land...
　　　　　　they were destined to live and have kids.

Ginger and Jill and Benjamin came
　　　　to bless our quaint, little farm—
　　　　it all resulted from giving her nod...
　　　　the beautiful, sweet Pamela Rose.

Then came grandkids, so far one girl and five boys
　　　　to fuss over and to spoil.

And now in the year of Jesus our Lord
　　　　fifty-one years since they met their lives have been
　　　　blessed and wonderfully filled...
　　　　Larry and sweetheart Pamela Rose.

How could one ever thank God enough?

Happy Birthday, sweet Pamela

Thank yous to those who remembered us:

　　We were humbled and honored by your attendance at our
birthday party. Jill told us in December that she was planning
a 70th for us. All we knew was that we were to be ready for
5:30 P.M. pickup on Pam's birth date. We didn't know who was
picking us up or where we were going. Were we surprised and
overwhelmed when we saw so many friends and family who came

to celebrate with us.

Pam and I had thought about opening presents before you left but the hectic pace precluded that so we thought we'd let you know what gifts we received: tulips and roses; Dove chocolate hearts; a huge patchwork quilt—that took hours if not years to complete (Alaskan motif with moose, bears, fish, mountains); ceramic chicken; Whopper candy; 70 year-old- birthday buttons; books (rhubarb cook book, outlaw tales of Alaska [have read some], stories from the heart book, a secret gift); 3 restaurant gift cards (Olive Garden—2— and BBQ Pit); Great Harvest bread basket and knife; cat calendar and bathroom guest towels; Alaska canned coho salmon and dip recipe (we ate pate 1-25/good); See's chocolate drops; wool socks and knee length socks; DVD's; Alyeska gift card; Colorado honey; organic pasta noodles; Texas red pepper ornament; a snoopy coffee cup and tons of wonderful cards. All those kind gifts were awesome but not to be exceeded by the power of your presence.

How thoughtful to remember us and to come share your time with us. For those brave souls who talked about our lives, it was so kind of you.

Some of you paid and/or tipped Gary the square dancing dude. Some spent an inordinate amount of money for food and supplies. Some toiled away for hours and/or days prepping, buying chocolate planes, making western cookies, cowboy colored picture and working to prepare and present the food (filling lemonade, etc.) and set up and takedown tables and other logistical things like vacuuming, setting up chairs for the next day's church service, removing-cleaning and returning table clothes, etc.

We had a blast. It was a highlight of our lonnnngggg lives!

Taking part in the square dancing added laughs and made it possible for Pam and me to do something she'd only previously dreamed of.

How do we ever hope to thank each for your thoughtful efforts and for coming to be with us?

Thank you so much.

You enjoyed the delights
of the first   18 years of
your life in   Oregon. I enjoyed meeting you in 1960
and
have
been
thrilled

for three times
that long,
54 years, that I
have   known
you...and   for those
same years that we dated...
and the 49.5   lived together.
HAPPY 72nd   B I R T H D A Y.

Congratulations   on all your years
of girl-   friending,   wifing,
mother-   ing, grand-   mother-
i n g .   Th a n k   you for
your   stable   commitment   to all   of those
and for   **your**   faithful
neighb'ring,   helping,   nursing, laundering,
cooking, gard'   ning and   **horsing around.**

You are absolutely the best. I love you.

Ginger's family

Ginger: Pam, I so love you—hope you have a great B-day.
          ♥ Ginger
Brad: Love you sooo much! Happy B-Day! Brad
Sarah: Happy Birthday! Hope you have a wonderful birthday.
          We love you Sarah

          P.S. Logan says Happy BDay as well.

Jill Rose

Dear Mother,

I have been incredibly blessed to have you as my mother. An incredible example of godliness and virtue, love, kindness and tenderness. And unlike many, I am able to call you friend as well. The last 30 years especially you have been a close tender friend. Thank you.

Happy Birthday Helen! I love you deeply and unwavering.

♥ Jill

Ben's family

Ben: Mom, Wishing you the most wonderful birthday. I am so thankful for each day of your life that I have been able to share. And I'm grateful for all the love you have given to me and my family. I am blessed for the parenting model of kindness that you modeled and Christian life you lived. I love you! Ben

Heather: & Reuben   Pam, Happy Birthday to a thoughtful and caring woman. I'm thankful for our friendship and our time together. May the next year be your best yet! Love you, bless you, Heather

Logan: Dear Grandma, Your the best grandma in the world!

♥ Logan

Preston: ♥

Love Cannon K

Lincoln: ♥

Karen Kendall

Dear Pam,

I hope you have a wonderful birthday. No one deserves it more than You. You are the most giving, loving person I have ever known and I pray that God richly blesses you on your special day.

This gift is to keep you through the winter blah's! Maybe you can see Spring around the corner with all its beauty.

Love you dearly, Karen

Jill Kaniut   **January 22 at 12:20pm**

Celebrating my mom's 74th Birthday.... So thankful for an incredible woman of God and the joy and blessings she is in my life and in the lives of all who know her. I love you Helen. I say have 'Coach' take you for a ride in that new truck.

Donna Helvey Happy Birthday, Sweet Pam!!!

Ann Baur Happy Birthday to her!

Lori Call Jones Happy Birthday Pam!!!

Zandi VanderHouwen Happy birthday!!!

Spring Boling Happy Birthday sweet Pam what a Godly woman you are.

Joanna Dicarlo Happy birthday to my other mom !!!! I hope y**ou have a great day !**

Eugene Greenfield Wonderful Lady! I hope she has a beautiful birthday !!!

Barb Robek Birthday Blessings!

Kelly Borror Happy Birthday to one of the loveliest women I have known in this lifetime. I love you Aunt Pam.

Lynne Wilkins Happy birthday aunt pam!!! Nice truck!!

Moira O'Bar Happy Birthday! Great picture!

Kim Miller Ingraham Happy Birthday, Mrs. Kaniut!!

MOTHER'S DAY

1)   2012

Happy Mother's Day

You are the **M** in Mother's Day…and
>   the **O**,
>   the **T**,
>   the **H**,
>   the **E** and
>   the **R**.

Mother, organized, thoughtful, heartfelt, effective and righteous.

Making our times hopeful and ever relevant.

That's our Mother, Pam

2)   2013 Larry

>   **P**ositively

>   **A**mazing

>   **M**other--

>   **E**ternally

>   **L**oving

>   **A**ngel

There are not enough beautiful and extravagant words to describe this auburn-haired, hazel-eyed beauty…especially on the inside. What a wonder and a treasure.
>   I love you.

VALENTINE'S DAY

Bio: grew up as Tomboy and flirt, health in gutter since DDT (college, childbirth), plethora of docs, alternative guys (Jerry—recommended by Karen Kendall) and Dr. Greg (recommended by Ken Royster), 2014 down to 93 pounds (no adrenals, no thyroid, flatworms in heart), always wants my help with spelling, octogenarians who received her letters nearly every week, incidents through the years

Qualities: thorough to a fault, righteousness/woman priority

MISCELLANEOUS

1)   Pam is more than an old violin…so much more. And priceless. Kind hearted, observant, considerate, great cook, mom, wife, homemaker, grandmother (crafts, make ups, Gingerbread houses), correspondent (writes 5+ octogenarians every week, long hand), counselor, role model, care giver, flower girl—green thumb.

Poem : *The Touch of The Master's Hand*

By Georgy ------ 17990 views

'Twas battered and scarred and the auctioneer

Thought it scarcely worth his while

To waste much time on the old violin,

But he held it up with a smile.

"What am I bid, good folk?" he cried.

"Who'll start the bidding for me?

A dollar, a dollar … now two … only two …

Two dollars, and who'll make it three?

"Three dollars once, three dollars twice,

Going for three" … but no!

From the room far back a gray-haired man

Came forward and picked up the bow.

Then wiping the dust from the old violin

And tightening up the strings,

He played a melody pure and sweet,

As sweet as an angel sings.

The music ceased, and the auctioneer,

With a voice that was quiet and low,

Said, "What am I bid for the old violin?"

As he held it up with the bow.

"A thousand dollars … and who'll make it two?

Two…two thousand, and who'll make it three?

Three thousand once and three thousand twice …

Three thousand and gone!" said he.

The people cheered, but some exclaimed

"We do not quite understand …

What changed it's worth?" and the answer came:

" 'Twas the touch of the master's hand."

And many a man with soul out of tune

And battered and scarred by sin

Is auctioned cheap by the thoughtless crowd

Just like the old violin.

But the Master comes, and the foolish crowd

Never can quite understand

The worth of a soul, and the change that is wrought

By the touch of the master's hand.

O Master! I am the tuneless one

Lay, lay Thy hand on me,

Transform me now, put a song in my heart

Of melody, Lord, to Thee!

– – – written by Myra Brooks Welch

Read more at Poem : The Touch of The Master's Hand http://www.turnbacktogod.com/poem-the-touch-of-the-masters-hand/#ixzz4bcBdwO8n

2) Poem Pam liked

Rest for the Weary

In the Christian's home in glory,
There remains a land of rest;
There my Savior's gone before me
To fulfill my soul's request.

He is fitting up my mansion,
Which eternally shall stand,
For my stay shall not be transient
In that holy, happy land.

Pain and sickness ne'er shall enter,
Grief nor woe my lot shall share;
But, in that celestial center
I a crown of life shall wear.

William Hunter (1811-1877)   John W. Dadmun (1819-1890)

3)   PAM'S POEM TO VICKIE BAER

"Thank God for You"

Thank God for you, good friend of mine,
Seldom is friendship such as thine;
How very much I wish to be
As helpful as you've been to me.
Thank God for You.

When I recall from time to time
How you inspired this heart of mine,
I find myself inclined to pray,
"God bless my friend this very day."
Thank God for you.

Of many prayer requests, one thou art
On whom I ask God to impart
Rich blessings from His storehouse rare,
And grant to you His gracious care.
Thank God for You.

114

So often at the throne of grace,
There comes a picture of your face,
And then instinctively I pray
That God may guide you all the way.
Thank God for you.

Some day I hope with you to stand
Before the throne at God's right hand,
And say to you at journey's end,
You've been to me a faithful friend.
Thank God for you.
--Author unknown

4) The Collected works of Billy Graham, *Angels, How to Be Born Again*, the Holy Spirit—Inspirational Press, New York, 1975

At one time no angels existed, indeed there was nothing but the Trinity…angels have the ability to change their appearance and shuttle in a flash from the capital glory of heaven to earth and back again…they do not possess physical bodies, although they may take on physical bodies when God appoints them to special task… God has given them no ability to reproduce, and they neither marry nor are given in marriage. (pg. 24)

David recorded 20,000 coursing through the skyways of the stars…Ten thousand angels came down on Mount Sinai…John tells us of having seen ten thousand times ten thousand angels ministering to the Lamb of God…armies of angels will appear with Jesus at the Battle of Armageddon when God's foes gather for their final defeat…they were commissioned not only to bar man's return into Eden, but with "a flaming sword flashing back and forth to guard the way to the tree of life. (pg. 25)

Angels speak. They appear and reappear. They are emotional creatures…our eyes are not constructed to see them ordinarily any more than we can see the dimensions of a nuclear field, (27)… God has given "His angels charge of you, to guard you in all your ways." (Jpg. 28)…they delight with us over every victory…(pg. 31)

LETTERS and MISSIVES PAM HAS PENNED

1)   Heather Kaniut

Heather,

That day at Outback how could I have known I'd be a part of your life…celebrating your birthdays, enjoying your food, sharing recipes, seeing your creativeness in decorating your home and gladly wearing clothes you took time to pass on to me. (like the sweatshirt I wore yesterday and the pants and slippers I'm wearing today)?

As the years quickly slipped by, I've seen you grant forgiveness, grow spiritually and do a superb job of homeschooling.

Thank you for trusting us with your children. Oh, how we love each grand boy.

You are a real trooper to work so hard to get well.

Now, you are off to another year of surprises and blessings with Ben at your side.

2)   Sarah Risch

"What If?"

by

Gramma K

March 2005

The Monday morning after Easter as soon as Sarah finished breakfast, she excused herself, thanked her mom for breakfast and took her dishes into the kitchen, rinsed them off and put them into the dishwasher.

Now she was free to rush to the back door. She yelled hello to her horse and then quickly looked down.

Yes, there was a small pile of gold nuggets. She couldn't keep from smiling as she said, "Thank You, Jesus" and picked them up and dropped them into her shirt pocket.

Back inside Sarah's mother reminded her to feed her horse then dress for school. "Sure, Mom," Sarah said.

In her bedroom she quickly placed the gold in a line. "Wow! Wow! Wow!," she thought. "If I keep saving these—some day I'll be able to buy mom and dad a newer car or the truck dad's been dreaming of."

As she put her barn coat and boots on, she began to think about the reasons for each gold nugget...

> I got myself ready for church yesterday,
> I ate nicely, like a lady at the Easter meal,
> I thanked them for the nice meal,
> I prayed,
> I did my homework.

"Sarah, Sarah, get up for school. It's Monday morning. Time to run feed the horse," her mother called.

From a very deep sleep Sarah finally came awake. She got out of bed and ran to the back door.

No gold nuggets!

Then Sarah realized she had been dreaming.

During breakfast Sarah told her mother about her dream and how real it seemed.

"I dreamed that every morning as God slowly drifted down sun, rain or snow...at your back door step, He also leaves a pile of gold nuggets—for each good thought, good deed or each prayer you have sent to heaven, from just the day before.

No one could see your pile but you.

You couldn't see anyone's pile.

And, I've been saving all my gold to buy you and dad a big, big surprise," Sarah informed her mother.

Reaching to hug her daughter her mom smiled a huge smile and said, "Sarah, if that were true, because you are such a precious, good child, we'd have your surprise very soon."

The End

Love, Gram

From Pam's 3 x 5 note cards and her college sophomore speech Sept. 21, 1961...which captures her love of animals...especially her horse.

Time…6 o'clock in the morning. She was just awakening…her eyes opened. After a few seconds, she realized that it was an early summer morning and that she had another busy day ahead of her.

She jumped out of bed and rapidly pulled her covers in place, then proceeded to clean her room.

She nearly slid down the stairs on her way to the kitchen where she found something to eat. Then from another room, she grabbed a milk bucket and left the house.

She and Rusty, her dog, played all the way to the barn. Her actions seemed to slow down now and take more meaning.

She pulled out an apple that had been hidden in one of her pockets and gave it to Duke in his stall. He smelled so good and his nose felt soft as she kissed it.

She left him now to call Candy into the barn, and then began an enjoyable time of brushing, milking and singing to her friend.

In a few seconds the cats' pans were full of warm milk.

Before long, she was in the house again, putting the milk in its place.

She turned to leave the house—but her mother had different ideas. So she vacuumed the stairways, helped with several other things and then was free to go. Before she left, she filled a sack with bread, cookies, took something to drink and then grabbed a handful of sugar lumps.

He was there waiting for her. Still so big, golden and friendly. As he ate his fresh hay, she cleaned his stall.

Then talking to him, she rearranged the cowboy pictures on the wall.

After a good brushing and Duke had been saddled, they walked out together onto the neighbor's range.

Coming on horseback to meet her, was her girlfriend. That whole day, until dark, the two girls found a million things to do together on their horses.

From 1951 to 1957, this was how I spent nearly all of my time.

In 1949, from a home in Portland my parents, 2 sisters, 2 brothers and I had moved to this 6 acres of land and 6 acres of water.

It was very enjoyable living there, just outside of Portland.

Youth from all of our churches took advantage of our water, outside fireplaces and Duke.

I was so in love with my horse and anything western that after my freshman year when I learned we were moving to a ranch, I really couldn't believe it.

But we did!

Our ranch of 569 acres is located just outside of Dayton, Oregon, on Red Hills.

I was lost at first, but gradually became accustomed to the big, equipment and large fields.

Now I could ride Duke all day long on our own property. My dream for so many years had finally come true.

But it was only a matter of months when my homework, school and church activities and steady boy friend seemed to take all of my time.

And then college came...I left the beautiful ranch and Duke and moved back to the city.

Surprisingly, it was a very wonderful year.

I was too busy to miss Duke very much.

Then summer came and I went home and worked on our ranch.

It was good to see the baby pigs, bottle feed the motherless lambs and spend time with Duke again.

The summer went so fast it seemed as if it were only a week long.

The evenings I spent singing to the stars, watching the lights of the valley and playing nurse to our many expecting mothers is now over.

The second year of another busy college life is now being experienced.

PAM SAYS or lollapaloozas

"Don't pay any attention to what I say; just figure out what I mean."   July 30, 2008

"I think we should hug and kiss and snuggle more…because we're almost dead."   Sept. 2010

Around 2012 Pam told Ben regarding marriage: Pam and Larry, "Sometimes we can't stand each other but we love each other."

"I heard some birds singing beautifully today. I don't know what they were telling their neighbors, but it sounded beautiful."

2013-14

June 6, 2014   Pam pronounced cupboard, cubbert. I told her, "There's no "t" in cupboard." She replied, "There is when I say it."

Today (Sept. 18, 2014) while eating breakfast I pointed out a woodpecker on the spruce behind the bay window—Pam's back was to the window. She turned, looked and said, "I wonder what time they get up in the morning."

Winter 2014-15   I wonder if those bugs flying around are having a convention or going shopping.

December 11, 2014   Pam asked, "Still like me?"

Larry said, "Why wouldn't I?"

Pam's response, "Lots of reasons."

Spring 2015   "I don't know how the spiders can build their webs so fast. I clean under and around everything in the bathroom. They like the secret hiding places where they build their webs and travel along."

May 23, 2016   I've been eavesdropping on the birds. They're very happy. I can't make heads or tails what they're saying. I weeded a little but I'm watching it to make sure I don't get myself in trouble. It's such a lovely day, I love being outside.

Nov. 28, 2015   After I told Pam I named you well by calling you Tundra Bunny, Pam said, "I want to stay active to live longer and accomplish as much as I can. I'm not sitting around smoking and watching TV."

Pam always stated in a joking way her desire to be busy: "I'm watching TV and eating bon bons."

Pam came into the kitchen where Sarah's cat, Trinity, was lying, stretching on her back on the seating bench and looking up at Pam. Pam said, "Hello. Are you begging?"   April 29, 2016

"When I went to college, I didn't care if I learned anything. I wanted to find a Godly man and to be a mother. I wasn't intimidated by not learning." 2/13/2017

1/25/2018 to Dr. Henry, dentist re: her lower teeth: "You don't need to worry what you tell me today about my teeth. I'll be happy with your input."

2/12/2018   Yesterday I couldn't do what I'm doing today. I never know but all I can do is do what I can do.

2/12/.2018   While eating lunch and her battle with chewing teeth Pam said, "If I could insert a couple of knives in my mouth, I'd do pretty good...and I'd look pretty feminine."

PAMMISMS

accessible	a-sess-able
acupuncture	aka-punter/puncture
breakfast	brecktruss
burglar	boogler
burglaries	booglaries/boogelries—3/2017

"That's as close as I can get with my Norwegian-Swedish-Italian-English heritage."

cauliflower	colleyflower
coyote	coy-ote
crisp cereal	chris cereal
cupboard	cubbert
had to	hadda
Havarti	have-y-art-y 2014+
kindergarten	kindygarten
Newt Gingrich	Newt Gren-rich
Norsemen	Nordsmen
other	ether/ever)

potatoes	ba-tate-os
record	wreck-ert
ruin	rune
secretary	sec-a-tary
salad	salat
Sioux	sy-you
tomorrow	to-mar-el
washing	worshing
Washington	Worsh-ington
You're welcome	welcome
window	windel
Wolfgang Mozart's Requiem	Rectum
wolf	woof

Pam's Christian Heritage

So, maybe I'll share what my young life was like…and other things.

Mother was born in Canada on a homestead. Out there, alone from other families or a city, before school age, mother accepted Christ. This gave her courage to walk by wolves to take her older sister to school. Her parents were not Christians. Liquor killed her father before I was born. Her mother got saved at 60 years of age while watching a church TV program. This grandmother was small and gentle, loved chickens and made about 12 kinds of cookies for each grandchild at Christmas.

My father was born in to a strong, loving Christian family—in Portland, Oregon. Father remembered seeing the first cars that came to Portland.

His mother took her cleaning to my mother's dry cleaning and sewing shop. So, that is how mother and father met…and where mother went to church for the first time about 1935.

His mother and father started churches in Oregon. Grandpa

gave out Bibles with the Gideon group. Until he died. Every morning they ate oatmeal and had Bible devotions together.

Until I was 13 we attended a huge, Portland Church of God—with grandpa and grandma and three other of their children and my cousins, then August camp meetings (sawdust on the floor—where I wore dresses mother made for me—and flirted with boys between services and while working in the cafeteria).

2nd chapter next week.

Now for Chapter II

Because my parents were Christians and I missed only a few Sundays attending church, it came natural for me to want to be a Christian.

One day while in my bedroom with my girlfriend my mother helped both of us understand salvation and so we both asked Jesus into our hearts at that time. Mother suggested we go up in front of the huge church the next Sunday so they would be aware of our intentions and so they could support us. That day older Christians did talk to me about being a Christian. That was very special to me.

I had good Sunday school teachers. Around 12 or so I decided to learn Bible verses…and began having daily devotions (reading the Bible, going over a prayer list, thanking God and asking for salvation, etc., of friends, neighbors, etc.).

By junior high I was part of a youth group at church, sometimes singing on Sundays a duet, etc.

There were about 6 churches of God in Portland. The youth meet for regular roller skating and every Nov. we had a retreat out of town. Those were wonderful, fun times and I did lots of flirting.

More later,

Love, Pam

Jan. 20, 2018   Some of my grade school, junior high and high school told to Ben and his family.

You have some Church of God history because my Great Grandfather Jordan moved to Oregon from Indiana and built the Failing Street Church of God in Portland. My grandmother Zeal handed out Gospel tracts when she was 16-years-old. Later after she married grandfather Earl, he handed out Gideon Bibles late in his adult life. Later on Holiday Park Church of God replaced the Failing Street church. My father's brother, sister and families all attended church together, except Velma who was in Nebraska. Dad and both Helens sang specials.

Sun bathing with Marcia…on our roof…in grade school and junior high, second floor on roof on hot, sunny days.

Walking to barn with my father—during those years, listening to symphony music as we headed to the barn to milk the two cows…and squirted milk into the cats' mouths…sometimes getting swished by a cow's tail, which was not pleasant when the tail was dirty. He played symphony music to please the cows.

Grade school age—with sister, made mud vases from the mud at the lake to dry in the sun, that neighbor boys always broke, Craig was nearby fishing by the bridge.

My father and brother Pepper had to clean all the mud and filth from our lake house which flooded, and they had to restore it. Mother had the buyers wait until it was completed.

One day our neighbor lady asked my parents if I could have Duke because she was getting a divorce and moving. I fed him carrots from time to time and was the likely candidate to receive him. He's been used to pull wrecked planes from the mountains. He was very gentle. My mom and dad stuck me on him with no training and I didn't know what to do.

Summer off to get Duke—opened fence, met up with Marlene on her horse Trigger…and not come back for as long as 8 hours, riding on their 200 acres. She would pull my horse bridle off and run off on her horse laughing. We took turns playing the Indian laying over the belly of the horse while the other one rode leading the dead Indian.

One day Marlene's horse Trigger pushed me into the outdoor fire pit in a field by her house.

I rode my horse from our house, up the street to the highway and the store, left Duke standing while I went to buy honey or something that had a coupon to get a free picture of Roy Rogers and his horse, etc.

In junior high I rode Duke up past the highway by our school to be in a parade. He was the only horse so I got a blue ribbon. Don't think any of my family came to see that.

By the 9th grade I was invited to sit and get a picture of me (which is upstairs) on Trigger, Roy Roger's horse. He was at that time the top actor and horse in movies. Marlene's dad was keeping Trigger for Roy who was in Portland and Marlene asked me if I wanted a picture with Trigger.

In junior high I worked cleaning cement off bricks my dad brought home from Good Samaritan hospital, he'd collected from dismantling the boiler room. My sister and I cleaned houses my father repaired in downtown Portland.

I began clarinet in the 4th grade, by junior high I rode the city bus to downtown Portland going into some tall building up to the junior high teacher's office for lessons.

I rode Duke on our big farm and heard a different sound in the ground at one area, told daddy. It was the best gravel in the county (and on the West Coast), but Meisel deceived my parents and took out only small amounts to make them think he was working the gravel pit but he had another pit and he didn't want my parents to sell to someone else.

PRINCE

Yard Moose from 2006 Kaniut adventures.

Friday, November 9 while Brad Risch and I were in Fairbanks, Pam had some excitement. She went to the barn to feed the animals (horse Prince, dog Diogenes, 6 chickens), she forgot to look closely for a moose or bear until she looked up and noticed a big, hairy long-legged ungulate. Pam had a dilemma in that she needed to get to the barn door in order to enter. She managed to avoid the moose (within 20 feet) and safely got into the barn.

Her next dilemma was leaving the barn to go into the house. The moose had migrated to the back deck, and Pam didn't have a key to the locked front door. She managed to get past the critter and into the house.

She went to the dentist with Tamara and came home to discover a Fish and Game guy (Rick Sinnott) coming from our neighbor to the east, and he asked her if she'd mind "if I put down a moose in your yard?" Evidently it had an injured ankle/foot and was trailing blood…probably from an encounter with a vehicle. He shot the young bull moose in our back yard and left after telling her someone would be by to collect it later.

About two hours later three people showed up and went to the back yard, dragged the deceased critter to our wood pile, along the lilac bush—depositing a trail of blood—and into the driveway where they loaded it up and left.

The next day a moose was on our front porch eating all that remained of the flower box flowers. All in all, a pretty moosey few days.

From 2011 Kaniut update

Pam keeps busy with her strawberry roan Appaloosa, white as a ghost which blends in well with our snow covered trees and lawn. And she enjoys her three chickens…is in "hog heaven" when she's outside in the barn, even mucking out the stall. Prince has the run of our yard year around.

Pam's Warrior Prince Casey O'Day

He came from Oregon. She took to him right away. It took me a little longer. And it took him a lot longer to get comfortable with me. He looked at me warily…stand offish and definitely wary. I assumed he'd been abused and equated me with that. It was probably two years before he felt at ease with me.

Pam thought about him all the time. She became conditioned to his presence and her routine included him daily. To say she loved him is understatement. She was always looking for him and hoping to see him—her very own strawberry roan Appaloosa—Prince K.C. O'Day.

He stood by the deck awaiting her when it was feeding time. He whinnied for her. He liked to laze by the fireplace chimney soaking up the reflected heat from the window. He loved being by Pam, either standing outside the bay window dozing inches from her where she lay on her seating bench or in the family room outside that window near her.

I erected a split rail fence on our northern and southern property lines to tie into our neighbors' cedar fences and we let him use the yard as a pasture.

In a way he was like a big dog. When we were outside with him in the yard, he commonly followed us around inches in our wake, often bumping into us as we stopped. He nuzzled Pam. Many a time it seemed he would follow us into the house. I even offered to replace the bay window for Dutch doors so she could open the top and let him poke his head into the kitchen. After he got used to me, he tried leaning on me but I reminded him that I should be leaning on him.

He was master of his domain, chasing moose from the yard then proudly prancing by the deck, nostrils flaring, tail aloft and mane flying in the breeze as if to say, "Look what I did. I'm protecting our yard."

He normally left her flowers alone until late in the fall when grass was scarce.

Periodically he managed to wander from the yard when his master left the gate open, a couple of times finding his way to the neighbors to the west and eating from their stocked hay. Once a lady driving by caught him and walked him into the neighbor's fenced yard.

From the summer of 1996 To March 23, 2015 she adored her pal. Twenty years. But when he reached 37 he was pretty tired and Pam decided in his best interests to relieve him of his agony and asked the veterinarian to send Prince to the Big Pasture in the sky.

Pam Writes

March was the third time Prince was affected by a neurological problem. His brain and legs changed. And, I don't think he could see much out of his best eye. And, his hearing had not been good for some time.

That Saturday morning when I looked out to check him, I could tell his back legs were at an angle. He was never able to stand normal after that morning and by Sunday evening he "walked" in circles, almost constantly…which left him sweaty and exhausted.

By Sunday night it wasn't safe for me to be in the stall…and quite a challenge for Sarah and the vet. The vet was sweating I think.

The vet was so kind. He came late Sunday night, staying until 1:00 AM—spent the night at his brother's home in town and was back Monday at 8 AM. The shots relaxed Prince some but in the morning the vet didn't' see enough change to put him through any more. The vet explained what would be happening next and even called for the "pickup" people who would take Prince away. They are the same company that Ginger used three times. Nice, thoughtful Christian people.

Because Jill notified people, Ben came. Was I ever surprised. Sarah and the vet got Prince out of the barn to the west side of he yard. Then Larry helped as Prince kept going in circles as the vet was trying to give him relaxing shots.

Prince went down for a quick second on his rear and got right back up. A few minutes later he went down on his rump, then plopped down his side next, then his heavy wonderful head lay on the old grass…and he never picked it up again.

I knelt by his head, getting to touch him for the last time. His eye lids moved, he wasn't completely still. I thanked God for him.

Inside Sarah invited me to go up to the barn where she cleans. What a thoughtful thing for her to do. As we left, a man came. He and Larry got on a conference call as the truck came for Prince.

People gave me flowers, ice cream, candy. I never expected all that love that day.

We have the best vet in the world. He even sent me a sympathy card.

I didn't realize how hard it would be on Larry. We miss Prince so very much .

Ginger was very supportive also.

Larry Writes

All that week Pam said she felt Prince's presence. I had a plan to paint a plywood cutout of him and station it at various places in the yard that he liked. I told her, "His presence is here. You'll see him again." And I proceeded to draw, paint and cut out his form for placement in the yard. Tuesday night I had the painted image (before cut out) leaning inside his stall so she could see it. When I talked with her in the house, I told her she should look outside if she hadn't.

2/15/2018 Pam's card to Tamie Hollingsworth re: her dog Nugget's passing
Even years after my horse died there are times when I'm sad for the loss and I really miss how kind and gentle he was—so easy to be around.

I still remember our first family dog in Portland and as a little girl I'd go into the garage when I was sad, sit on the steps and he'd come up to me. I'd hug Rusty, sing to him..and cried while with him.

Meese in the Yard

About March 5, 2005 yours truly was going to cut his hair on the back deck. Requirements included our old Sears electric clippers and an extension cord. I walked to the barn to fetch a cord and spoke to Prince, the white roamer of the yard and eater of the grass at 4800 Natrona. He was by the barn door and I asked the trusty equine how he was doing. Then I noticed a yearling moose calf about 25 feet away, about halfway to our shed and said to the moose, "How ya doin', pal?" The moose looked a little embarrassed and had that "what should I do now?" look in his eye as he backed up and wondered what to do.

I walked into the barn, grabbed the cord, walked to the house and plugged it in. Pam said, "There's another one by the garden." And sure enough, there's mom walking along behind our cedar rail fence. I told Pam it might be a good idea for me to put the horse in the barn.

About then the mother cleared our fence east of the shed and walked the path by the tree house straight to the deck. She was within 5 feet and I was wondering if she planned to come aboard and attack me. But her ears were not laid back and her hackles were not up. I think she intended to walk around the big birch tree with the I Love Rose valentine sign on it and eat branches.

I told Pam, who was standing in the doorway, to go inside if the moose came any closer. Thinking the moose might retreat if I turned on the clippers, I did so. *Bbbbrrrrriiiiii.*

I don't think the clippers had any effect on her, but all of a sudden a white tornado erupted from out of nowhere, ripping from my right to my left and attacking the moose.

Prince zipped at her, she spun on her rear hooves and fled, the horse on her tail until she cleared the fence. Then he turned down the path from the shed to the barn and met junior head on. Junior wheeled and cleared the fence faster than mama.

Then Prince trotted around to the right of the deck with his tail arched and snorting. I said, "Good for you, Prince. You da man. You protected your property."

PAM'S HAPPY MARRIAGE RECIPE

A Happy Marriage
From the kitchen of…
Ingredients

Gentle, kind, love:	lots
Minimum:	5 hugs each day
1 "Love you"	each day
Spoonfuls:	touches and cuddles
Cupfuls:	"Come on, baby, light my fire."
Whenever needed:	"I'm sorry; please forgive me"
Every day:	"You're my doll baby."
	"You're my stud muffin."

Bring to boil, let simmer daily

Oven temperature:	heartful
Time:	life
Serves:	2

--Pamela Diane Kaniut

PAM'S FUNERAL ARRANGEMENTS

Pam and I drove to Chapel by the Sea Feb. 16, 2018 to pick up forms for the funeral service.

Pam talked about her funeral arrangements on October 3, 2011:

At Chapel by the Sea—view for all—3-4 PM

    Ice cream and waffle cups—celebrate

    Chocolates

Planted next to hubby at Klatt cemetery

Songs: "In Sweet By and By" end service with "May the Good Lord Bless and Keep You"

No preaching

Celebration and happy time: "If the words of this song and my life aren't good enough, a sermon won't be."

2012 Larry's Dream

I awakened from a dream June 9, 2012 at 3:30 A.M. I had been dreaming of what I'd say if presenting at Pam's memorial service and I tried to remember and write it down.

I chased her four years until she caught me. I became her reclamation project. Her parents wanted nothing to do with me. Might turn out to be like my parents, alcoholics. And that wouldn't fly with the Timmonses. Who could blame them? But I persisted. She saw something in me.

She rescued me. Brought me into her world. Just a plain, beautiful, smiling young woman at Warner Pacific College—a tender, thoughtful and considerate lady who treasured life in spite of the bumps in the road. After fifty-one years of dating and nearly 48 years of marriage, she has me almost house broken. And it hasn't been easy.

I once wrote our son Ben to "cherish your wife." Oh, how I wish I could have lived up to those words every day. Cherished Pam every hour. Never upset her. Made each day a joy for her. She deserved the best.

How can you describe specialness? Perhaps a terrific synonym is Pamela. From the way she made do in the way she dressed; prepared flower arrangements; took cakes, pies and flowers to neighbors; made the bed; fixed meals; cared for her children and grandchildren; made others feel at ease; spelled and pronounced words like woof, windel and warshing; smile; "paired" her stockings for wash with clothes pins; used a spoon for every jelly on the table; refused to admit defeat especially in her poor health; gardened and "flowered"; cared for her animals; arranged furniture; shoveled snow; loved being outside on "lovely" days; wrote countless letters and cards of encouragement and support; and developed lasting relationships.

Her smile covered some of it.

She was top drawer.

Countless are the lives she's touched with her grace and goodness. Angel in disguise doesn't even come close to capturing her charm, charisma and Christ-like demeanor.

Index

The following folks contributed to our memory book.

Jane Adams	Pam's nephew's friend became ours; visited AK parent's cemetery
Gene Amondson	college freshman classmate, 1960, Warner Pacific College
Joyce Amstutz	college classmate of Pam's at Western Oregon
Lynette Baer	neighbor girl grew up with our girls from 1974-1989
Vic and Vickie Baer	40-year neighbors
Leslie L. Baldwin Jr.	Okie, nephew of church friends the Ertz family
Brenda Bauer	church friend in the late 1960's, husband Bob played basketball
Gordon and Karon Best	neighbors in 1970
Beth and Rick Biel	neighbor girl married Larry's nephew then moved to Washington
Alison Bjornseth	church friend, step-daughter of Tom Kucera, our neighbor three years
James Buchanon	Larry's student and friend from 1980's
Dan Bylsma	Larry's student and family friend from 1970's; AK AWANA director
Cliff Carrell	church-family friend, we attended college with his brother

Julie Chase	
Mary Ruth Curtis	AK pastor's wife, church friend, choir director (Gary and Brad's mother)
Naedene Maslen Duran	niece of Pam's brother's
Janice Eckard	friend who purchased one of our books in 2000's
Michael G. Edwards	
Jeanne Ellsworth	Pam's nephew's wife's mother
Carole Espedal	Pam's aunt
La Vonne Ertz	church friends since 1970's, Larry fished for Ralph
Sue Francis	family friend
Chuck and Norma Fuller	friends from church camp since 1970's
Jody Garcia	family friend beginning in 1975
Weston Gray	family-college friend, dated Pam's sister in late 1960's
Eugene Greenfield	church youth-friend, son of Tom Kucera
Cindy Hamman	neighbor girl-family friend from the 1980's
Bonnie Hemry	family friend, daughter-in-law's mother
Tamie Hollingsworth	family friend and neighbor
Rita Hughes	church friend since 1980's
Kim Miller Ingraham	Jill's school friend, family friend from 1980's
Kyle James	dad Tony was Larry's student-athlete, family friend since 1970's
Jill Kaniut	second daughter of Pam and Larry
April Tincher Kaufman	Larry's student, Jill's friend and our family friend from 1980's

James Jody Keasler	church friend and Larry's student in 1970's
Jeff Kliewer	our son's college friend and roommate later
Gary Kendall	friend and son of our first Alaskan pastor, since 1966
Karen and Hershel Kendall	family friends since 1970's; aunt-uncle of Gary Kendall
Vivian Lenore Kralman	Pam's mother-in-law; Larry's mother
Louise Kucera	2nd wife of Tom
Jean Kurtz	Larry's teaching colleague at A.J. Dimond since 1966
Quency Light	church friend since 1980's
John and Delores Lindeman	teacher-coach, friends from Oregon, 1965
Pastor Steve McCoy	pastor and family friend since 1980's
Donna Meeks	family friend since 1966
Sherry Merchant	account colleague with Larry in writing, family friend since 2000's
Peggy Merritt	Larry's highly respected teaching colleague and family friend
Carole and Sonny Miller	Larrry's former student, neighbor
Linda Monsarat	son-in-law's mother
Roy and Joyce Mullen	Larry's student-athlete, graduated 1971, close family friend
Pat Murphy	neighbor whose girls grew up with ours
Lorin W. Myers	college classmate at Warner Pacific College from 1960-1963
Alice Nobel	family friend from church
O'Neal	church friend since 1980's

Michele Gibbens Otten	family friend; Larry's former student
Cal Pappas	Larry's teaching colleague-family friend from 1985
Helen Partlett	aunt of neighbors Chris and Derek Snyder
Dann L. Pierce	Larry's student-wrestling manager; family friend since 1966
Les and Izzy Pohlzin	son-in-law's grandparents
Marcus and Ingrid Reese	neighbors
Brad Risch	Son-in-law
Ginger Risch	daughter
Sarah Risch	number one granddaughter
Lynn and Donna Roumagoux	Larry's teaching colleague and family friends since 1967
Kay Shively	friend from publishing who moved to Alaska (2000's)
Jennifer Hughes Silverdale	church youth and family friend from 1980's
Marilyn Skau	son's receptionist; family friend since 2003
Jaylin Skrukrud	neighbor girl to the east; sweetheart
Al Smay	Larry's student-athlete from 1966; family friend forever
Gary LaRay Smith	high school buddy of Larry's; drove to college together in 1960
Janel Knisley Smith	church-family friend from 1970's
Laura Lee Smothers	Pam's sister-in-law; Larry's sister
Christopher Alexander Snyder	neighbor boy since 1970
Virginia Snyder	grandmother of neighbors Chris and Derek Snyder
Kim Speegle	Pam's niece

Dale Steele	family friend, church family, pastor
Wes and Ione Steele	church friends since 1960's
Lynn Stuart	family friend of Pam's since 1950's
Katie Goerisch Sturgell	neighbor girl two houses west, moved away 19890s
Rod Taylor	Steve Phelp's nephew, church friend
Randal Terry	Larry's student-athlete, close family friend from 1971
David, Pam, Cherlyn and Ryan Thibault	helped with church canteen, family friends
Hazel Timmons	Pam's mother since 1942
Gene and Jeannie Wallace	church friends since 1980's
Emma Wilson	Pam's brother's mother-in-law
Ronni Woolrich	church friend since 1980's
Debbie Yingling	church friend since 1980's

Books by Larry Kaniut

Alaska Bear Tales

More Alaska Bear Tales

Cheating Death: Amazing Survival Stories from Alaska

Danger Stalks the Land: Alaskan Tales of Death and Survival

Some Bears Kill

Safe with Bears: Bear Conflict Survival

Bear Tales for the Ages: From Alaska and Beyond

Alaska Air Tales

Brachan: A Soldier's Secret Mission

Trapped: An Alaskan Romance

The B.G. High School Flashbacks

Heavenly Rose, Angel in Disguise

Instant Sourdough

Alaska's Fun Bears

www.kaniut.com

www.ingramcontent.com/pod-product-compliance
Lightning Source LLC
Chambersburg PA
CBHW071005120626
46546CB00003B/939